Start Now
SUCCEED

Making College Count for Career Search Success

LATER

Patrick S. O'Brien

 South-Western College Publishing
an International Thomson Publishing company I(T)P®

Cincinnati • Albany • Boston • Detroit • Johannesburg • London • Madrid • Melbourne • Mexico City
New York • Pacific Grove • San Francisco • Scottsdale • Singapore • Tokyo • Toronto

D1122789

Acquisitions Editor: Pamela Person
Developmental/Production Editor: Mardell Toomey
Marketing Manager: Sarah Woelfel
Manufacturing Coordinator: Dana Schwartz
Internal Design: Kevin Lison, Graphic Management Corporation
Cover Design: Paul Neff Design
Compositor: Graphic Management Corporation
Printer: West Publishing

I(T)P® The ITP logo is a registered trademark under license.

Printed in the United States of America
1 2 3 4 5 6 7 8 9 10

International Thomson Publishing Europe
Berkshire House
168-173 High Holborn
London, WC1V7AA, United Kingdom

International Thomson Editores
Seneca, 53
Colonia Polanco
11560 México D.F. México

Nelson ITP, Australia
102 Dodds Street
South Melbourne
Victoria 3205 Australia

International Thomson Publishing Asia
60 Alberta Street #15-01
Albert Complex
Singapore 189969

Nelson Canada
1120 Birchmount Road
Scarborough, Ontario
Canada M1K 5G4

International Thomson Publishing Japan
Hirakawa-cho Kyowa Building, 3F
2-2-1 Hirakawa-cho, Chiyoda-ku
Tokyo 102, Japan

International Thomson Publishing Southern Africa
Building 18, Constantia Square
138 Sixteenth Road, P.O. Box 2459
Halfway House, 1685 South Africa

Library of Congress Cataloging-in-Publication Data
0-324-01540-2

This book is printed on acid-free paper.

Preface

College courses prepare students for doing well *on* the job, but provide little preparation for how to get the job even when addressing the career search process. Similarly, non academic books about job hunting emphasize resumés, the interview or sometimes both topics but leave out much information needed specifically by college students *entering* the job market. *Start Now. Succeed Later. Making College Count for Career Search Success* fills in this gap. Students need to be informed about how to build a well-rounded college experience that will make them successful in getting their careers started once out of school.

This book, whether used alone or as a supplement to another, will help students build life skills that will assure future career success. Students will learn that the best jobs do not go to the best-dressed candidates or those with the longest list of club memberships; the best jobs go to the candidates who can demonstrate a wide range of important skills. Those skills are clearly defined by use of the acronym COLLEGE which stands for the seven winning characteristics needed for a successful job search: communication, organization, leadership, logic, effort, group skills, and entrepreneurship. *Start Now. Succeed Later. Making College Count for Career Search Success* develops each of the concepts, helping students realize their importance and how their own skills might be deliberately cultivated over the course of their college experience.

Personal Insights

I have written this book based on my experience as a student, a new hire, a general manager, and an entrepreneur. In addition to my personal experience, I have drawn heavily on the experience and insight of many business managers as well as recruiting and career center professionals who see students in the job search process every day. These professionals from respected companies like GE, Microsoft, PricewaterhouseCoopers, and Procter & Gamble, know what leads some students to great jobs and others to great frustration. Every chapter includes their comments from the front lines. Students should read these comments thoughtfully; they have been carefully selected to provide valuable advice based on many years of experience.

Personal Progress

Every student will find reading *Start Now. Succeed Later. Making College Count for Career Search Success* to be a very personal experience since it continually challenges readers to evaluate their own progress and prospects in the career search. To help in this effort, each chapter includes brief exercises in which students must consider the choices they have made and will make. These exercises make the book a living document to be consulted again and again throughout college and the job hunt.

The philosophy of this book is quite simple: every student can choose to become a more valuable and desirable future employee. I've tried to make those choices as straightforward and clear as possible. Students tell me they like the writing style: good old-fashioned straight talk, both from me and from recruiting and placement professionals.

I'm convinced every college student will finish this book with a better under-standing of how to approach career success. It is only a matter of making the right choices—based on information provided here—and then having the desire and discipline to stick to those choices.

Pat O'Brien

Pat O'Brien

Acknowledgements

In developing this text, we are indebted to so many people it is virtually impossible to give all of them credit. The contributions of recruiters and career center professionals were critical to the book's "real world" aspect—something that we believe will give it strong appeal to students from all types of universities. I would like to thank Trish Rasmussen, who was tireless in conducting these interviews and capturing the content from them over a period of many months.

We also appreciate the contributions of the following professors who reviewed the text and who offered numerous helpful suggestions and comments:

G. Jay Christensen, California State University, Northridge
Sandra Ihle, University of Wisconsin, Madison, Wisconsin
Dana Loewy, California State University, Fullerton
Lisa Tyler, Sinclair Community College, Dayton, Ohio
James B. Wehrley, High Point University, High Point, North Carolina

Special thanks go to Steve Mott, an exceptional writer who helped craft the tremendous amount of content in the book into the cohesive and approachable piece that it has become. His thoughts, writing expertise, and commitment all played a major role in the final product. It would be fair to say that I couldn't have done it without him. Thank you, Steve.

Finally, a special thank you to my friends at South-Western College Publishing. From Amy Villanueva who had the initial vision for the project to Pamela Person who evolved it and brought it to life, and Mardell Toomey who guided us skillfully through the development and production process, it is truly an exceptional group.

Table of Contents

SECTION 1
Introduction to Success

The Purpose of College

Why are you here?

The question is not *What is the meaning of life?* or *Why are you on this earth?* We'll leave those questions for another forum. The question is simply this: *Why are you in college?*

At times college may seem like a crazy idea. In college you spend thousands of hours stuffing your brain with ideas and facts, many of which seem to have no practical application in your life and few of which you will remember past the end of the semester. You sacrifice the 2–5 years of work experience and income you'd gain if you skipped the lengthy academic experience. Or you attend college at night after toiling all day in a full-time job. You or your parents spend $2,000–30,000 per year for the privilege of taking classes you sometimes don't enjoy and occasionally don't even attend. You often live with a total stranger in a room with less charm than a mediocre hotel. And finally, in college you work hard to prepare for life after graduation, but you receive no guarantee that you'll get a better job or have a better life than if you didn't attend college.

Here You Are

Despite all this, students across the country are attending universities, colleges, and community colleges in record numbers. About two-thirds of high school graduates now make the choice to go to college. Including you!

Why each individual chooses to go to college is, of course, a personal matter, but like any other decision it is generally made as follows: I'll follow the path that will lead to the best overall result. Most students picture their long-term outcomes, including career, family, and lifestyle, as more favorable after attending college than they would be without college. If you're in college of your own free will, you probably made the decision to attend with this basic expectation.

So whatever goals you have set, whether general or specific, you probably hope that college will help you achieve them. *Start Now Succeed Later* will not attempt in any way to define or shape your goals. Your goals are your business. Whether you are looking forward to a successful career as a stockbroker, day-care center operator, fashion designer, or actor, this book can help you make meaningful progress toward meeting your goals. Even if you have no idea what field might be right for you, the pages that follow can help you build important skills that are valuable in almost any career, or in further study beyond college.

Give Me a Choice

Every college career is wonderfully unique, but each has one common characteristic: at some point it ends. When yours ends, there's no better situation to be in than to have a number of outstanding choices available to you for life's next step. This book will shed light on what you can do now—right now—to broaden your choices for your post-college years. Getting a great job after college is not the only reason to attend school, but having a great job waiting for you when you graduate is a nice option—even if you decide not to pursue it. Not having any options, on the other hand, is rarely desirable. You could probably learn more about that by talking to the one in three college grads who don't get a first job after college that requires a degree, or one of four 25-year-olds who for financial reasons still live with their parents.

Finding Balance

College is supposed to be fun, you're thinking. Why ruin it with a lot of pondering about the future? True enough, college provides an environment of freedom, people, and possibilities unlike any other. College can be fun, and should be a happy time in your life. Most important, however, college—even night school—can be both incredibly enjoyable and very productive at the same time. What you learn from this book is highly compatible with having great friends and great times. Better yet, what you learn from this book can lead to a *lifetime* of great opportunities, great learning, and great fun.

Of course, achieving career success is no magic act. Reading this book alone will do nothing to help you land a great job after college. You'll need to put significant effort into your future, make tough decisions, and set priorities and stick to them. But relative to the rewards you will reap after college, you'll find the sacrifices well worth the effort.

Let's get started.

Defining Success

There is no single definition of success. The concept of "success" is inherently personal. A hilltop mansion and fleet of luxury cars might be a dream for some and of little interest to others. The ability to make a meaningful difference in someone else's life may mean more to some than anything money could buy. And each person's individual definition of success can change significantly over time. For instance, one's high school fantasy of a career on Wall Street may by the age of 30 turn to a yearning for the simple life in a small town.

What we consider a "great job" often includes a nice salary, but it also involves working with interesting people, encountering new and different challenges, and achieving a balance with one's personal life. Your own definition of success relies entirely on your values and interests, not on a national standard, the images of late night infomercials promising fame and fortune, or the expectations of others.

A Long Journey

However you measure success, it is best described as a journey; it is not defined by a single event. Achievement occurs not in great bounds, but in small incremental steps. No one picks up a guitar for the first time on Monday and signs a lucrative record contract on Thursday. Thousands of small victories must be won first, through practice, lessons, networking, and more. Indeed, many of the hottest baseball "rookies" are 25 or older and have played literally thousands of backyard, little league, high school, college, and minor league games before they advanced to their first at-bat in the majors.

Now let's explore the concept of the distance between success and failure. It may seem like a huge chasm for people who have not yet achieved their dreams, but in reality the gap is often quite narrow. The difference between someone who lands a role on what turns out to be a smash TV hit and the last person cut in the casting process may be quite small. The person making the decision may not even be able to explain rationally the one or two things that set one outstanding candidate apart from another. The difference between success and failure in a Super Bowl may come down entirely to one swing of the foot by a kicker who spends 59 of 60 minutes standing on the sidelines. For Olympic athletes, the difference between the glory of a gold medal and the anonymity of a fifth-place finish is rarely more than a few seconds or inches. Job success works the same way. Making or missing one's sales quota for a particular month often comes down to one's ability to close just one more sale.

Putting this into career perspective, the difference between someone who lands the dream job and someone who gets a second-tier position may be hard to distinguish. The final decision may have ridden on one or two answers in the interview process, a key piece of experience, or even something as intangible as the perceived "work ethic" of the candidates. Obviously the gulf between the class valedictorian and someone who manages only a 1.9 GPA is significant, but few competitions are so clear cut. In most cases the selection process for a great job or slot in a prestigious graduate degree program involves two or more equally smart, hard-working, capable individuals. What made the difference in who landed the job may have been just a few choices made during the college experience.

Choices Matter

A key point: Success much more often hinges on choices than luck. In fact, choices generally matter more than raw potential. Unfortunately, you can't look into the future and tell which of the hundreds of decisions you're making today will make the big difference 5, 10, or 20 years from now. So what's the moral of the story? Every choice may be important, so make every one of them count.

Perhaps the most important choice you can make while in college is to "make the extra effort." It may sound corny, but just a little extra effort in academics, extracurriculars, work experience, or even all three, may give you that 10% boost in the interview process where the best are separated from the rest.

While giving extra effort is an essential first step, there's more to it. It is not just that you put forth the effort that matters; it's where and how you apply that effort. When you finish this book, you'll better understand where and how to focus your energies to create the kind of skills and track record that will open doors for you at graduation. The book will present concrete examples of smart choices you can make starting today, plus the invaluable perspectives from the people who know best—directors of some of the nation's most successful college career centers and top recruiting professionals at some of the world's top companies.

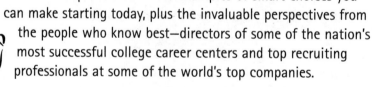

No matter how you define success remember: You control your chances of achieving success through the choices you make from this day forward. *Start Now Succeed Later* can help you understand how best to take advantage of the opportunities available to you as you plot your course toward success and satisfaction during your college career.

Analysis

What are the three best and three worst choices you made last week?

Best

_____

_____

_____

Worst

_____

_____

_____

SECTION 2

The College Success Process

It's Interview Day

Only a handful of humans have walked on the surface of the moon. For the rest of us, that sensation of bounding around in low gravity is difficult, if not impossible, to imagine. The same applies to the interviewing process. More people have been through interviews than have tromped the lunar surface, but the idea is the same—until you've done it yourself, it can seem like quite a mystery.

Eventually you will get to know the interviewing process quite well, whether it takes place on campus or elsewhere. The more interviews you experience, the better you'll understand how it works. But even after you become a veteran job candidate, you could be missing an important side of the story—the process taking place on the other side of the interview desk. Even partial insight into the recruiter's point of view is quite enlightening, and that knowledge can be a source of considerable advantage as you sit in the interviewee's chair.

The Recruiter's View

Recruiting is not as easy as it seems. You may think that a recruiter just sits there and talks to students all day and picks the one that's best for the job. What's so hard about that? Believe it or not, it is difficult to pick the right candidate, very difficult. To see why, appoint yourself the interviewer for the moment.

On a typical day, as a recruiter visiting a campus you will interview, individually, from 12 to 16 students. Each will be relatively clean-cut, bright-eyed, and enthusiastic. Each will look you in the eye and tell you that they really want to work for your company and that he or she is the ideal candidate for the position you offer. They'll say it with their resumé. They'll say it with their words.

Many students will even rehearse answers to the questions they think you may ask. They'll be ready. They'll deliver airtight, highly polished answers. They may even practice on videotape and receive coaching to make sure that they look as sincere and capable as they possibly can. When asked if they are highly motivated, 15 out of 16 will tell you that they are. When asked if they are strong leaders, 13 out of 16 will respond yes. When you ask them if they're effective in a team setting, at least a dozen will tell you that they are, and say it with complete conviction. "I'm a great communicator," at least half will say. Or, "I get along with everyone."

In short, you'll find that most of the candidates you interview will claim to be perfect for the job, and many will fit your general mental image of what you're looking for. It's genuinely difficult to distinguish the contenders from the pretenders, the leaders from the pleaders. You'll meet many people who seem extremely qualified, in every way, and many who don't interview well but have great grades, or vice versa. You'll see youthful enthusiasm, bright smiles, and raw potential. You may even interview a few people who remind you so much of yourself that you want to hire them immediately.

Hard Work

The process gets harder as the day wears on. After interviewing three or four candidates, you have a favorite you want to hire. After seven or eight, you have trouble keeping people straight in your mind. After ten, you're tired of hearing rehearsed and empty answers. By the end of the day, you're actually longing to return to the office and your stack of unfinished paperwork! When you look at your list of candidates the next day, you really don't know with 100% confidence who would be the right choice. Recruiting is just plain hard.

Recruiting is hard work, and it's much more pressure-packed than one might expect. As the recruiter, you need to pick winners. You need to recommend those students with the best potential, who will do well in subsequent interviews, and who will reflect well on you once they're on the job. You certainly don't want to be known company-wide as "the one who recommended that loser in product design." A string of poor-performing selections might even cost you your job. You must make smart choices.

There is a lot of pressure on the person doing the recruiting, particularly in an organization like ours where we spend a great deal of money on training. We typically spend about $30,000 per new hire so it's very important that we bring in people who are a good match with our organization. The fact that it is so important encourages a very structured approach to the process. We want to get as much information about the individual as possible and also want to make sure they have a lot of information on us, truly understand what we do, and are excited about the opportunity we are offering.

Jeannie Maibe
Director of US Consulting Recruiting
PricewaterhouseCoopers

10

To be successful as a recruiter, you need to sort through 16 students to find the one or two who deserve your personal stamp of approval to take the next step, whether that next step is additional interviews, personality testing, aptitude testing, or a job offer.

Try and put yourself in the employer's shoes. If you were hiring for this position what questions would you ask, what skills would you be seeking? This allows the interviewee to anticipate questions and consider what skills/experiences the question would allow them to focus on.

Christine M. Sullivan
Director, Career Services
Salem State College, Salem, MA

Making the Recruiter's Job Easier

Knowing what you now know about the challenge facing recruiters, doesn't it make sense to tailor your interviewing techniques to meet their needs and to make it easy for them to identify you as the right choice? Hopefully you're starting to realize that to stand out it takes much more than a nice suit, a firm handshake, and enthusiastic responses.

To seem better than and different from your peers, you need to be better and different. You need to do more than just tell the interviewer that you possess the skills they seek. You need to really have those skills and be able to prove it through clear, concrete examples of how you used them in meaningful ways. Then amid even a day full of students' unsubstantiated claims about their awesome abilities, your hard, cold evidence will stand out in the best possible way.

Later in this book we'll explore the specific Winning Characteristics that potential employers will be seeking, and the ways you can build those skills and demonstrate your mastery of them.

Analysis

Have you ever interviewed candidates for a job, organization, or any other opportunity? If so, what percentage of the candidates told you that they were well qualified?

_____

_____

_____

_____

The Proof Is in the Story

The ideal candidate for a job as a mortgage banker would have years of experience as a mortgage banker, a proven track record, and hundreds of satisfied customers. But a recruiter who's interviewing on campus to fill that job is not looking for that kind of candidate—college students just don't have that kind of experience. What the recruiter seeks is someone who can become a top performer.

The recruiter knows there is a specific set of skills that will be required to become that top performer. Given that, she has to make a choice. She can hire students who appear able to develop these essential skills on the job, or she can hire students who have already exhibited these skills in their college careers. The first option obviously carries greater risk. Even a top student who demonstrates a strong desire to learn and improve may come up short in one or more important skills. Hiring someone who is unproven in the area of leadership, for instance, may work out perfectly, or it may be a major disappointment. There's no way to know. The lower-risk choice, of course, is to hire students who can clearly prove they possess the skills required to do the job.

I will ask candidates to elaborate on specific skills from either their course work or previous work experience. Group projects are especially useful in this way. A candidate can highlight specific skills (analytical, organization) as well as discuss teamwork, leadership, and project management examples.

Adelaide T. Auble
Manager, Corporate Capital MA Program
KeyBank

If someone has performed in a certain way in the past, they are more likely to do so in the future. This is the basic idea behind the concept of behavioral-based interviewing—a very popular approach to job candidate selection today.

Prove It

As the saying goes, talk is cheap. While one may truthfully believe and claim to have the communication skills, attitude, and other key elements necessary for success on the job, an unsupported claim just doesn't mean much. An interviewer may talk to dozens of students at several schools to fill just a single position, and many students will claim to have the right stuff. The students who will stand out as the best candidates will have proof—meaningful stories that focus on how they learned the desired skills and put them to work during their college careers.

Your own stories will serve several important functions. First and foremost, they prove that you possess the key skills that lead to success. Secondly, they demonstrate your meaningful involvement in a variety of areas and activities—this in itself is an attractive characteristic. Finally, stories are memorable. Your description of how you pulled together a team of volunteers to conducts AIDS awareness seminars will be much more memorable than one of your peers reciting a rehearsed answer about "working well with others." Sticking out in the memory of a recruiter is a necessary first step to getting the job.

We use behaviorally anchored interviews and bio-data to assess a candidate's past experience and present activities. This approach is based on the belief that past behavior and demonstrated results are the best indicators of future behavior and success. For example, if you have smart people who have taken initiative and shown a flair for creativity in the past, the probability is high they will continue to do so in the future. Here again, we have invested heavily to make sure we have validation studies to feel comfortable this approach works to identify a stronger overall applicant pool from which to select the people who will succeed in our culture. The best way for an applicant to succeed in our process is to have examples of specific things they did or accomplished that will help differentiate them from other smart people.

Bill Reina
Director, U.S. Recruiting, Training & Development
Procter & Gamble

Your stories need not, and should not, relate only to what you accomplished in the classroom. They can describe how you developed and used skills in extracurricular campus activities, community organizations or events, hobbies, and work experience of any kind, including internships. And they do not need to fit exactly what you might consider to be a "conventional" success story. They simply need to communicate clearly to the recruiter that you own the specific skill about which he is questioning you about. That the stories need to be true should go without saying.

Think about the various events in your life. Maybe you ran a publicity campaign for a friend's art show. Maybe you started a fan club for the seniors on the basketball team. Maybe you organized an exciting new ski club trip to Colorado and created a successful fundraiser to pay for it. Maybe you started a personal fitness company to help pay for school, offering personal training to area residents. Maybe you spent a few weeks of your summer following a favorite band and writing a series of articles for your campus or local paper about your travels. All of these would be great success stories to share with a recruiter. If you're getting the idea that the experiences do not have to be painful, laborious projects, you are correct. The stories simply need to present specific examples of how you utilized important skills.

The key here is the student's record of past achievement. More and more, employers are taking a what-have-you-done approach over a what-can-you-do when it comes to selecting new employees. It is very important that students recognize that their potential future performance will be evaluated largely on their prior experience. In order to develop an impressive track record of accomplishment during college, it's also important not to start your senior year. The process must begin much sooner—as early as freshman year, in fact. Become involved. Have a positive impact.

Dr. Robert Greenberg
Director, Career Services
University of Tennessee-Knoxville

Resumé Fluff

Many students make a natural, but costly, assumption about their activities and how they use their time. Consider the case of Jake, who by junior year had amassed a list of 17 memberships in clubs, honorary societies, and associations. His resumé looked like the Greek alphabet—Phi Kappa This, Sigma Sigma That. Jake was confident that being a member of so many organizations would make it clear to recruiters that he was involved and capable. But Jake never did anything in these clubs; he rarely even attended meetings after he joined. Jake hit a brick wall in the interview process. When recruiters asked him about his achievements in these many clubs, he had nothing to say—he had no stories. His value to potential employers evaporated entirely when he was asked to talk about his successes and how he contributed to the progress of the organizations on his resumé. Being a member of just two organizations, and taking roles of responsibility in both, would have been a much better strategy for Jake.

> *When it comes to interview questions, I really don't have any particular favorites. In behavior-based interviewing, the direction of the interview is determined by how the questions are worded (e.g. "describe to me ..." or "tell me about a time..."). I don't use any one set of questions. I want to make sure, in essence, that the questions that I ask the student are varied. I will use this technique to make sure I am focusing on that individual in terms of what they have previously accomplished. For example, I might ask someone to describe your role as president of [a particular organization].*

> *Peter Bowen*
> *General Electric Corporation*

Being a joiner rather than a "doer" is a common mistake—one to avoid! Another trap that some students fall into is joining only the top organizations on campus and believing that making even minimal contributions to "top" groups will suffice. Unfortunately, most recruiters who come to the school may not even recognize these clubs as special. Even if they do, they're interested in a student's impact on the club or group, not merely one's membership in it. As you select your activities, remember that what matters is what you do in an organization, not what organization you choose to join.

By the way, high school stories count too. Any solid examples of your abilities should be included in your interview ammunition, whether they occurred in college or before. Just make sure there is a balance between past and current accomplishments. If you were the biggest fish in the small pond of your high school and you have not continued to build your portfolio of success stories in college, interviewers may question your ability to achieve in a fast-moving, competitive work setting.

In any case—high school or college—remember that stories are your best means to sell yourself. A mere list of clubs and honoraries is not likely to impress anyone, except perhaps your parents.

Analysis

What are your three biggest college success stories thus far?

_____

_____

_____

What are you currently doing that could be a great success story?

_____

_____

_____

A Model for Success

Builders follow blueprints. Engineers have detailed technical drawings. Auto designers start with clay models or computer renderings. Having a plan or model greatly improves the chances of creating something that looks and works as desired.

This chapter is about the college success model, a model of the skills and experiences recruiters value and seek in graduating students. By clearly understanding the kinds of credentials employers are looking for, you'll be much better prepared to assemble those skills and experiences during your college career. Following this model will equip you with a long string of success stories to share with recruiters, the kind of true stories that lead to second-round interviews and job offers.

The college success model is based on Winning Characteristics. Winning Characteristics are a collection of skills that will take you wherever you want to go. So what are these Winning Characteristics, the specific traits that impress recruiters? You'll explore each in depth in the coming chapters, but let's start with a quick overview.

An Important Spelling Lesson

Developing and demonstrating the Winning Characteristics will spell success and opportunity as you embark on your career search. The Winning Characteristics also spell "COLLEGE"—literally.

Communication Skills — the ability to effectively exchange information and ideas with others, in many settings and through different media

Organizational Skills — the ability to effectively manage a great deal of information or multiple projects and priorities

Leadership — the ability to bring people together to achieve a common goal

Logic — the ability to think through a difficult problem to a positive solution

Effort — the attitude and energy to do what it takes to achieve meaningful goals

Group Skills — contributing to the success of a team

Entrepreneurship — the willingness to innovate and take on risk for the purpose of an uncertain reward

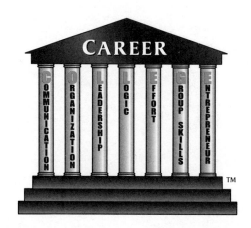

The skills you list are all important and repeat what employers constantly tell all of us—once you have gained a basic level of competency in an academic area, it's everything else outside the classroom and inside of you that will count. These transferable skills will not become obsolete over time, like "technique" information may; rather, you have the opportunity to improve on your skills in the complex interactions demanded in the rapidly changing work environment.

Dr. Wayne Wallace
Director, Career Resource Center
University of Florida

As the diagram above suggests, the Winning Characteristics are the core attributes that create a valuable candidate in the job market. You conceivably can build a solid background without excelling in all of these categories, but if more than one or two of the pillars are missing, your chances for success may be a little shaky. Further, trying to land a great job based entirely on strength in one attribute is like balancing a roof on one pillar—expect a large crashing noise to follow.

Section 3 discusses the seven Winning Characteristics in detail. Your ability to learn and practice these skills and demonstrate them to potential employers will largely shape your success in the job market, or as a candidate for a graduate degree. But there's more to the college success model—it's a three-dimensional model, where the key skills are built on a three-part foundation. These three elements provide the opportunities for you to develop the skills employers seek as you progress through your college career.

A Sturdy Foundation

The first piece of the foundation is academics. There's no big surprise here—you need to achieve some level of success in the classroom to demonstrate your thinking ability to employers. On a more basic level, failing grades often lead to an untimely departure from campus and very limited job opportunities.

We're looking for performance as a company. We want to be the best in the world at what we do. Given that, a student's GPA is tremendously important. An outstanding GPA means you're top of the class. That's the kind of student we're trying to attract to meet our corporate goals. Practical experience plays a role in this area, as well. We'd rather have a student with a 3.75 and experience than someone with a 4.0 and no involvement outside the classroom.

John Zweig
Corporate Employment Manager
Apple Computer

The second piece is extracurricular activities—what you do out of the classroom. It includes clubs, honorary societies, and organizations of all kinds, on and off campus. These activities present the most effective—and the most often ignored—opportunities to build key skills. The opportunities here are limited only by your own creativity and energy level.

> *When looking at a job candidate's resumé, I like to see a diverse person who is involved in various clubs and organizations. However, I don't just stop there—I look at the total person. I mean, they may belong to the Society of Women Engineers, they may belong to the National Society of Black Engineers, or they may belong to a society that deals with mechanical or electrical engineers. Depending on the individual, I like to see that the resumé kind of holds together and that where the individual is going makes sense for the total person.*
>
> *Peter Bowen*
> *General Electric Corporation*

The final piece of the foundation is work experience. Work during college is a fact of life today for most college students, but few realize its full potential. You can earn much more than a paycheck through work experience, even if the job has nothing to do with your intended career field. It's all a matter of how you approach your responsibilities.

When evaluating prospective job candidates, we tend to look for variety in their backgrounds. How many different and meaningful things have those candidates done in their lives? To what groups or organizations do they belong? What, if any, work experience do they have? There is really a broad spectrum of activities we consider. We want someone who has taken a multi-directional approach throughout life. The more variety, the better.

Allan Jones
Manager, College Recruiting
American Management Systems, Inc.

This three-dimensional approach to college will be explored thoroughly in Section 4. Like the Winning Characteristics, building on all three of these experiences creates a more attractive, more well-rounded package for recruiters than strength in just a single category.

Starting Right Now

Think about where you are right now. Where have you focused your attentions thus far in your college career? Very few students develop a truly balanced set of skills and experiences. Most tend to stick to their strengths. Talented students worry most about academics and fail to get involved in clubs and activities. "Natural leaders" may spend all of their time working with their various organizations while their grades inevitably slide. The truly well-rounded college grad is definitely an endangered species, which means that building balance in your own experience will make you stand out for all the right reasons when interviews roll around.

Now is the perfect time to take a look at your own personal college record, exactly as it stands today. Looking at it using the model at the end of this chapter may shed some light on where you need to work a bit harder. Many students fail to take an honest look at their strengths and weaknesses until the spring of senior year, much too late to make any major changes in how time is spent. The sooner you examine your progress, the better chance you have to end up with a great job—not just any job, but the job you want.

Simply understanding the college success model sets you apart from the vast majority of your peers. Recent graduates consistently describe that they have no idea what recruiters seek outside of good grades. Using the college success model to guide your efforts gives you a big head start in developing a profile interviewers will immediately recognize as high potential. While your classmates are devising ways to puff up their resumés, you'll simply be choosing the best among your many success stories.

The model is simple, but don't confuse "simple" with "easy." You'll need to make some tough choices and sacrifices to assemble a killer set of Winning Characteristics. You'll have to pay more attention to how you spend your time than most students do. You'll need to wander out of your comfort zone now and then. It's not easy, but it will take you where you want to go.

Where Do You Stand?

Before you continue to the next chapter, take a few minutes to recap your current status in the light of the college success model. This will act as your starting point for all future efforts.

Academics

GPA by Year: Fr _____ So _____ Jr _____ Sr _____

GPA in Major: _____

Extracurricular Involvement

Club/Organization	Offices Held	Most Significant Accomplishments
_____	_____	_____
_____	_____	_____
_____	_____	_____

Work Experience

Jobs Held	Most Significant Accomplishments
_____	_____
_____	_____
_____	_____

Across Career and Company Boundaries

All jobs are the same.

Butcher, baker, candlestick maker. Tinker, tailor, teller, teacher. Publicist, programmer, performer, principal. All the same. Every one. Sure, people in these positions spend their time differently in the day-to-day activities they perform. And they have specialized expertise and training. And they work in different environments, perhaps in different kinds of clothing. Nonetheless, almost all employment at its core level involves a small number of commonalties, things that make all jobs more similar to each other than different.

The commonalties that link all jobs boil down to customers and problems. Customers come in many different shapes and sizes. They may be bosses, consumers, other businesses, government, children, parents, or even animals. But there's always some constituency to satisfy, some customer to please. And every job also comes with its own set of challenges. The challenges may be minor and brief, or agonizing and persistent. But problems must be solved for the progress to be made that allows an organization to survive and, hopefully, thrive.

In short, all work comes down to two fundamental realities:

All jobs involve satisfying customers.
All jobs involve solving problems.

A job in which no customers are satisfied and no problems are solved will not be a job for very long.

During the interview process, I also look for problem-solving skills. We try to ask questions in the interview that get beyond whether or not they possess critical-thinking skills. We want someone who is going to be able to solve problems. Every company, every organization has problems. Big or small, you need people who can creatively solve them.

Michael VanGrinsven
Associate Director of Recruitment & Campus Development
Northwestern Mutual Life Insurance

Common Issues, Common Skills

If all jobs are the same in these two important ways, what are the implications for the job search and recruitment processes? The answer lies in skills. Satisfying customers and solving problems often require some degree of technical or industry-specific knowledge, but they also require fundamental skills—skills that are common across all kinds of jobs and types of work. These basic skills—the Winning Characteristics introduced in the preceding chapter—are invaluable in every job and will often be more important than technical knowledge in solving problems and pleasing customers. Certainly in the long term those people with the most complete set of Winning Characteristics will be the most likely to be assigned top projects, advance through promotion, and have a choice of future career moves.

Students in highly technical fields sometimes disagree with the idea that skills are more important than knowledge, but experience proves it to be true. Consider engineering as an example. An engineering student with an outstanding grasp of his or her academic program will typically land a good job coming out of school even with mediocre leadership, communication, or other key skills. This is a simple matter of supply and demand—there are more engineering jobs than there are well-qualified engineering students, and you can't be a good engineer without strong technical knowledge. Because of the shortage, a candidate doesn't have to be perfect to get an entry-level job. However, the truly great engineering jobs, the ones where competition is strongest, generally go to engineering students who are more well-rounded, demonstrating both technical ability and Winning Characteristics.

Once on the job the disparity continues. Employees who show entrepreneurial ability, organization, and the other Winning Characteristics are more likely to be promoted, selected for fast-track programs, and offered the best projects. The engineer who can communicate not only with his peers, but with non technical clients will be highly valuable to the organization. And anyone who consistently works well in a team environment will be more likely to advance than those people who make teamwork difficult.

I'm sitting on a U.S. Department of Labor and Job Corp panel, and we just developed a list of competencies that students need to be successful in the Information Technology sector. Quite frankly, I don't see that they're too different from the skills required to be successful in any other field—things like communications skills, problem-solving skills, working with other people. They are basically the competencies that are required for any field.

Anne Gordon
Skills 2000 Program Marketing Manager
Microsoft

So a broad mastery of the Winning Characteristics can be a deciding factor in landing and succeeding in a technical job. But that's definitely not the end of the story. The same concept applies to artistic or creative jobs. A highly creative marketing student may land an entry-level job as associate copywriter in an ad agency. Inevitably, though, the associates who are best able to work with others, handle sticky customer interaction, solve problems under tight deadlines, and take the lead on important group projects will be the most sought by account managers and clients.

The Recruiting Challenge

If you were recruiting engineering students, would you be more likely to hire a student who had strong technical skills only, or one with a full range of Winning Characteristics? Not a tough question. Like it or not, engineering is only part of what an engineer does. Writing is only part of what a writer does. Physical therapy is only part of what a physical therapist does.

That's a major reason why companies spend thousands of dollars to interview students all over the country. If all that mattered were academic skill and technical knowledge, a transcript and grade report would do the trick. But because the ultimate goals are to satisfy customers and solve problems, the personal and interpersonal characteristics that can be evaluated only through face-to-face meetings matter a great deal.

The importance of Winning Characteristics is positive news for all students intent on getting a great job. These are skills that can be learned, practiced, and demonstrated through concrete examples. Even if you do not have a 4.0 in your major, you can still be a standout if you apply the effort to build these essential skills. And don't despair if you're not sure about what specific job you want. These skills apply to *all* jobs, because as we've seen, all jobs are the same in some very important ways.

Simply put, the college success model works for any and all students and career fields because every career involves solving problems and satisfying customers.

Analysis

In your current or most recent job, who are your customers?

_____

_____

_____

What problems do you (or did you) solve in that job?

_____

_____

_____

Skills Aren't Inherited, They're Learned

Natural athletes. Great communicators. Born leaders. Some people have all the luck.

It often seems as though we are surrounded by people who were born with DNA preprogrammed for exceptional grades, entrepreneurial achievement, and effortless success in all endeavors. These people make everything look so easy. They have all the skills you're working so hard to develop, and they got them with no effort at all. It's hardly fair.

Yes, some people do get lucky. Some people are clear and engaging communicators from the age of ten. Some gravitate with complete ease to positions of leadership. Some can sing. Some can solve impossible math riddles in seconds flat. In fact, almost everyone has some kind of gift, whether it is athletic, physical, or mental. But very few people, none in fact, are born with all the skills necessary for success. Your best high school teacher, for instance, might have been naturally intelligent and a skilled communicator, but he probably had weaknesses in other key skills. If he seemed to be a natural in every skill, there's surely more to the story.

What you probably don't see is how hard these seeming "naturals" have worked to develop the skills that seem innate. A senator who brilliantly delivers an important speech at the Democratic National Convention has likely honed that skill by giving hundreds and hundreds of speeches over dozens of years, at the PTA, city council, state assembly, and elsewhere. And she probably spent hours practicing in front of advisers or on videotape as well. For the overwhelming majority of people, regardless of background or career, skills come through experience and hard work, not luck.

As you measure yourself against the seven Winning Characteristics, you'll undoubtedly find that you need more work in most of them. Almost everyone does. Here's the good news: college represents the single best opportunity you'll ever encounter to build the skills that will serve you throughout your career (and in life in general). Why is college such a prime breeding ground for Winning Characteristics? The obvious answer—that you can take classes to build the skills you need—only goes so far. Most of the key skills are not taught in college or anywhere else. The real answer can be traced to these two unique elements of the college experience:

- The wealth of opportunities for participation and experience
- The low cost of failure

Do It All

Even the quietest college campus offers literally hundreds of opportunities for involvement and growth. Between class projects, extracurricular activities, internships, part-time jobs, volunteer activities, and everything else that revolves around a campus, college is the ultimate Winning Characteristics factory. At virtually every school, the number of opportunities to build your skills is limited only by your creativity and energy level. Plus, you have more discretionary time as a student. You may consider yourself quite busy now, but when you look back on your college career from the chaos of raising a family while working 50–60 hours a week in a full-time job, you'll realize how much time you have today.

Learning Lessons

College is a great place to try new things. Maybe you've never spoken to a group larger than your hometown Bible study class, but realize you need to develop this aspect of your communications skills. There are innumerable opportunities to address large groups on campus, from classes to clubs to student activities. So you get involved in one of these opportunities and find yourself speaking to 150 students and faculty members. When you do, it doesn't go very well. You lose your place in your presentation, stumble over simple phrases, or forget one of your main points. You're frustrated and a little embarrassed. But guess what? Despite your discomfort and disappointment, you're lucky to have had this relatively risk-free experience. You may be frustrated, but that's about the worst of it.

Consider the alternative: you're in your second year as a salesperson for a software company. You're asked to address a trade association. You've never spoken to more than 20 people, and here's an auditorium of 444 faces staring at you. Now that's pressure. If you whither at the podium, it may cost you potential sales, damage your reputation, or limit your opportunities for advancement. Speaking to a dozen large groups on campus almost guarantees a stronger result in the same situation after graduation. If nothing else, you will be more relaxed.

A Big Choice

In college you face a choice: to avoid your weaknesses or turn them into strengths through conscious attention and practice. Facing your weaknesses is the more difficult but much more productive option. Regardless of the specific skill, you'll definitely improve with practice.

As you explore the specific Winning Characteristics that follow, be sure to consider how you can build these skills in the high-opportunity/low-risk campus setting. You'll be glad you did.

As to the question as to whether skills are learned or inherent, this is one of the great questions of the ages. Therefore, it's very difficult to answer. However, in my opinion, an awful lot of learning takes place. For example, it is possible to learn the skills necessary to become an effective leader—developing organizational skills, setting short and long-term goals, or managing group activities. No one is born knowing how to do these things. I think the reason many people assume someone is either a born leader or not is due to the concept of "charisma." This is a natural trait. However, not all charismatic people are effective leaders and vice versa. There seems to be a higher percentage of learning associated with being an effective leader.

Dr. Robert Greenberg
Director, Career Services
University of Tennessee-Knoxville

Analysis

What are the two key advantages of attempting to learn new skills in college (versus after)?

_____

_____

_____

SECTION 3
The Winning Characteristics

Communication Skills

The ability to communicate effectively in a wide range of situations is the first of the Winning Characteristics, not just in this book, but also in overall importance. You may be able to overcome a lack of knowledge in a particular area, a weakness in organizational skills, or a shortage of leadership experience, but lacking strong communication skills greatly and immediately reduces the number and types of jobs for which you may qualify.

In simplest terms, communication is the ability to deliver and receive information effectively. The basic components of this skill are reading, writing, speaking, listening, and persuading—whether on computer, in person, in documents, or on the phone. As technology evolves, so too does the number of ways we communicate with one another, but the fundamentals do not change. You provide information and ideas to others, and you receive information and ideas from them. Communication is at the core of every business enterprise. You simply cannot function with any degree of success without communication skills.

> *Communication skills are critical to success within our organization. Oftentimes, our people are on small teams and they need to present information orally to those groups. We also have a lot of people who travel from one Lockheed operation to another, not only locally but throughout the country, making presentations, etc. Therefore, it is really critical for us to be able to communicate effectively.*
>
> *Howard Roe*
> *Manager, University & Career Center Relations*
> *Lockheed Martin Astronautics*

Why is communication so important? You might say that "no job is an island." Even positions that seem to offer a high level of autonomy and independence require cooperative effort with others. Almost every job involves working on one or more teams, either within a department or across the organization. There are quality teams, customer service teams, account teams, new product teams, among others. We'll talk a lot more about teams under another Winning Characteristic, group skills. Teams are an important part of modern business, and working effectively in that environment is essential to advancement.

Probably the most important skills we look for during the interview process are communication skills. We look for the ability to interact and share thoughts and ideas relative to the questions that we're asking. Also, we look at an individual's ability to pose questions aimed at learning more about us. It is the basic element of engaging people and interacting with people in an effective way.

Michael VanGrinsven
Associate Director of Recruitment & Campus Development
Northwestern Mutual Life Insurance

Beyond teams, there is a more fundamental need for communication—customers. In every business there is some kind of customer. It may be an internal customer, perhaps a manager in another department. Or it may be a more traditional customer, an external entity or person. If there is no customer there is generally no job. In some cases your only "customer" may be your boss, but that makes it no less important to provide responses to his or her needs. Regardless of the customer's identity, meeting her expectations requires clear, timely, and accurate communication, both directly with the customer and with others involved in helping the customer. Meeting needs and solving problems are all about communication.

In companies where the customers are external, sales people take the lead role but they are far from the only people with customer contact. A good customer will become a "partner" of sorts and interact with product development people, operations managers, package design specialists, financial analysts, and others in the organization. Communication skills are, therefore, at a premium for students in all disciplines, headed for all kinds of jobs. And in sales, the premium placed on communication skills is even higher.

Constant Communication

Communication skills are used constantly in every organization. They allow learning, teamwork, creativity, and efficiency. Consider a typical morning in an entry-level position. You start the day by checking your voicemail messages that have arrived from your boss, a co-worker, and a client. When you return the calls, you reach voicemail for your co-worker and answer her question. You talk to your client who has a problem with a previous order and needs a quick solution—you commit to check it out and call back soon. The message from your boss reminds you to have a report finished and posted on the company intranet by 10 A.M.

Then you check your e-mail. Again, they come from a mixture of internal and external associates. E-mail is very efficient because it can be used any time of day or night to send short, fast messages. However, it does require great clarity in writing so the recipient does not have to "decipher" your message. That means understanding with whom you are communicating and adjusting style, terminology, and content to fit that person's knowledge level and perspective.

After e-mail, you attend the 9 A.M. morning meeting with your boss and team members. There you learn about a new product being introduced and what that means for you and your clients. You ask several questions to clarify the offering, being careful not to dominate the meeting or ask redundant questions.

Then it's back to your desk to assemble the report your manager requested on an upcoming customer project. This report starts with a one paragraph summary of the project and supplies supporting detail on several key points. You're submitting the report to your boss, but you know he may share it with the manager of another group that is involved in the project, so you write it in a way to be clear for both readers.

Then you get on the phone to track down the answer to the question your client raised on voicemail about her order. And so your day goes, a continuous cycle of asking, listening, writing, responding. All of these activities represent communication in different forms, but with a common goal—getting the job done by sharing information.

Getting Technical

Much of modern communication takes a digital format, the language of computers. E-mail is a fundamental business tool, and Web sites are an important communication vehicle for many firms. Reports once written by hand or typed are now universally done on computers and transmitted not on paper, but through e-mail and company networks. Computer skills, therefore, are a must in almost any job.

An interesting phenomenon has developed regarding computer skills. Anyone over the age of 25 now assumes that anyone under 25 is a computer wizard. How could you not be, growing up with Nintendo and Sega, constant Web surfing, and computers in almost every home in the country? Because of this assumption, a lack of computer skills can be a major shortcoming in your job search, and on the job. Oddly enough, if you were 45, you would likely be "forgiven" for marginal computer literacy. But at age 22, a job candidate will simply be expected to have solid computer skills.

Without some knowledge of computers, you're going to have a difficult time getting a job anywhere.

Anne Gordon
Skills 2000 Program Marketing Manager
Microsoft

Computer skills are definitely not just for computer science majors anymore. Cornell University recently completed a study that indicated that 74% of employers who recruited at the school for all fields would like to see some level of computer proficiency. These recruiting companies identified five key capabilities they prefer:

Word processing
Financial spreadsheets
Basic graphic design/page layout
Basic database management
E-mail

Many other firms would like to see the ability to write HTML code (the programming behind most Web sites) as well. You don't need to be able to create a 60-page multifaceted Web site, but basic knowledge of HTML code can certainly be a plus.

Computers Are Everywhere

You would be hard-pressed today to find a field where strong computer skills wouldn't be a benefit to you. If you are considering performing arts, you may think a computer would be irrelevant to your life. It might be—but probably not for long. Let's say you get your degree, head for New York, and land a few minor roles in off-Broadway shows. You're making a living, but just barely, and find a couple of years later that you've basically stalled on the on-ramp to the road to success.

You're approached by the owner of a theater where you've performed. She thinks you're bright and energetic and perfect for the job of managing her theater. You're intrigued with the idea and interview against three other candidates for the position. They can't spell computer and you're an expert on one. You can help in strategic planning, ticket inventory, payroll management, and profitability projections, and can create clever new marketing ideas on-line at minimal cost. You can also effectively communicate at a professional level without the help of a secretary because of your word processing skills. You're hired! On the flip side, let's say you make it "big." If you do, you'll be running a business. With agents, public relations people, financial advisers, and hectic schedules, life will get very complicated very quickly. Computer skills will be a major asset in helping you manage your successful life.

Developing the Skills You Need

It should be very clear that communication is a key skill set. So how can you develop the proficiency employers expect? As with almost any skill, the answer lies in experience and practice. The good news is that the college environment is perhaps the best training ground you could ever hope for when it comes to communication—there are truly limitless opportunities to build your skills.

What we hear from employers, over and over again, is that new college graduates simply have not developed effective communication skills. From my experience, I find this is the #1 difficulty reported by employers of recent graduates.

Dr. Robert Greenberg
Director, Career Services
University of Tennessee-Knoxville

A key first step is to evaluate your existing skill level. Maybe you're strong in computer skills, but dread giving presentations in front of large audiences. Maybe you're a great listener, but struggle with writing. Wherever you're starting from, you'll want to concentrate your efforts in the specific areas that need the most work.

Unlike many of the Winning Characteristics, communication can often be improved by taking a class, whether it be public speaking, business communications, or basic composition. Of course, it is never enough to simply take the course; to really improve skills takes hard work. It means pushing yourself to not just pass the course, but to internalize what you learn for future use.

Beyond coursework, communication skills can be built through involvement in campus groups. As a leader in a Greek organization, student government committee, or the ski club, you will have many opportunities to interact with others, speak in front of a group, or submit reports. As with classes, the point is not just showing up so you can put it on your resumé, but working hard to develop the skills you need.

Work experience, especially an internship, can also provide the practice you need to develop effective communication ability. An internship in your chosen field is best of all, of course, but even working in the registrar's office a few hours a week will help you build computer expertise, interpersonal skills, and basic writing abilities.

Communicating about Communication

Your personal presentation is very important in the job search and interview process. Interviewers will be looking for every available clue about how you communicate, both how well you present information and how well you listen. Do you truly hear the question before you start your response? Are your responses to questions comprehensive and well-organized or random rambling punctuated by "uhh" and "you know?" Is your resumé clear and concise? Are your questions about the recruiter's company direct and succinct? These clues may tell only part of the story about your communication skills, but they are all the recruiter has to go on in the confines of an interview. The moral of the story here is that proper preparation—thinking about how you might answer questions before the interview and practicing interviewing—are outstanding ways to build interview success.

For us, the interview is probably the most powerful way of determining whether or not students have good communication skills. We assess whether or not they ask good questions and if they use appropriate body language when necessary. We also look at whether or not they are able to articulate their backgrounds quickly and if they are able to summarize their involvement in key projects. Can they summarize their statements in an understandable manner, or do they ramble on aimlessly? The interview process is very effective in answering these questions.

Chuck Davis
Keane, Inc.

Be prepared to tell recruiters about the classes, extracurricular activities, or work experience where you developed and practiced communication skills. Describe your most difficult communication challenge or how you effectively delivered bad news to a group and kept them motivated. Show samples of your writing. Any type of Web site development work or on-line resumé are definite plusses. If you have an on-line HTML-based resumé with links to a thesis paper or other work that demonstrates your skills, you'll definitely make a positive impression. Wired Resumés (www.wiredresume.com) is a great, student-friendly way to build an HTML resumé.

In short, the more ways you can demonstrate your ability to communicate with a wide range of audiences and via a wide range of media, the more valuable you will seem to a recruiter and your manager. As with all of the other Winning Characteristics that follow, remember that it is never enough to simply possess a skill; you must be able to make it clear to your potential employer that that skill really is well developed. The more specific you can be about your communication abilities, the better.

Analysis

How would you rate yourself on the computer skills employers seek (based on the recent Cornell study)?

	Poor	Fair	Good	Very Good	Excellent
Word processing	❑	❑	❑	❑	❑
Financial spreadsheets	❑	❑	❑	❑	❑
Basic graphic design/page layout	❑	❑	❑	❑	❑
Basic database management	❑	❑	❑	❑	❑
E-mail usage	❑	❑	❑	❑	❑

Organizational Skills

It's a complex world out there. Being organized makes it a lot more manageable. The second Winning Characteristic is organizational skills. Being organized may not have the same dynamic ring to it as being highly creative or eloquent, but for many employers, organization is a very big deal.

If you look at almost any job description on the Microsoft Web site, almost all of them have organizational skills as a required competency. If you don't have that ability, you can get lost quickly in all the new technology. The industry is moving a lot faster than it used to. We move very, very quickly at Microsoft, and as technology is playing a bigger and bigger role in every other sector in business, other companies will be moving more quickly as well.

Anne Gordon
Skills 2000 Project Marketing Manager
Microsoft

Being organized means being able to manage effectively a great deal of information or a number of complex projects at once. It involves prioritizing, shifting focus at a moment's notice, managing details, meeting deadlines and commitments, and developing reliable plans to accomplish your goals.

On the job, exercising strong organizational skills may be the only way to keep a project on budget and on schedule. To be involved in the higher profile and more interesting projects (meaning those that will lead to greater visibility and opportunity), an employee must consistently demonstrate the ability to handle the details and juggle multiple tasks. That's why recruiters will make a concerted effort to identify candidates who are able to keep track of responsibilities, schedules, files, names and numbers, customer account information, and the other tools of the trade.

The Value of Being Organized

Organization has a very real monetary value in the marketplace. Think of an employer who has 40 customers or 40 key projects to manage. She knows from experience that a well-organized, highly skilled employee can handle 8 complex projects simultaneously. Less organized people seem to struggle with any more than 5 projects each. That means hiring 5 organized people or 8 less efficient paper chasers. Obviously she will prefer to hire the organized people, even if she has to pay them slightly more—the savings are immediate and significant.

New hires need to be able to organize their work to get it all done. They're multi-tasking all the time. It's not like they work on one project and have one boss. In an interview, we want to know how they have managed their time, managed multiple activities, and how they've handled it when an unexpected event came up. We really get into what they have specifically done to prove that they have the skill.

Jeannie Maibe
Director of Management Consulting Recruiting
PricewaterhouseCoopers

The average worker spends hours each week looking for information or other essential materials. Every hour spent looking means one less hour solving problems, making new contacts, and generating revenue. Furthermore, an organized person typically makes fewer "unforced errors," as they call them in tennis. Mistakes can be very costly both in terms of money and time. And let's face it, someone with six-inch stacks of paper scattered across and around his desk is more likely to lose track of something that really matters. Even those seemingly "sloppy" people who seem to know where everything is may suffer skeptical opinions from a tidy boss.

Another important element of the organization equation is being able to maximize your results through smart use of the resources available to you. If you know where to find answers, tools, and the people who can help make things happen, you will improve not only your own productivity, but also that of your staff and fellow team members. Every family, dorm,

and club has one or two people who can be turned to for answers. You want to be that person in your future work environment.

But how important is organization really? Let's say you work for an electronics manufacturer that is launching new super-light portable CD players. There are 43 people on the team from engineering, R&D, purchasing, product development, marketing, sales, legal, manufacturing, marketing, etc. The entire launch must be executed in six months to get the product to the store shelf before the holiday selling season. Every day of delay may cost $100,000 in sales. The critical path project schedule is an inch thick. There's simply no room for missed commitments, delayed paperwork, or backtracking to fix mistakes. If you were the manager of this key project, what kind of people would you seek in staffing the project? Keep in mind that if anyone drops the ball on a key step of the process, causing a four-day delay, the manager won't receive his bonus.

Another quick example: You're a rookie at a local stock brokerage firm, and your quota is to open 6 new accounts each month. After 3 months you're way ahead of the target, the envy of your peers, with almost 40 accounts. But now the market takes a stumble and you're getting calls from 15 clients or more every day. You can't find their account information, remember their investment objectives, or manage your callbacks. You start to hear frustration in their voices, and some even take their accounts elsewhere. What will that tell your boss (or your clients) about your ability to manage 100 or 200 accounts? Boring as it may sound, organization definitely matters.

Building the Skill

This concept—getting organized to achieve stronger results—will be a familiar one for most students. Managing a schedule of 5 or 6 classes, each with multiple assignments, tests, labs, and papers, plus a part-time job and other commitments can seem like a monumental organizational challenge, and it is. On the job, the challenge is similar, but the stakes may be a bit higher (perhaps a promotion, raise, or bonus).

Fortunately, the habits you develop in college can translate well to the work world. A great starting point is to establish a 9-to-5 mentality; dedicating the hours of 9 A.M. to 5 P.M. strictly to academics. If you fill all non class time with consistent study sessions, instead of naps, TV, computer chat time, and other diversions, your evening hours will be remarkably free. In interviews this discipline will make a great example of your organizational ability and can have a very positive impact on your lifestyle, too. If you work during the day, take a slightly modified approach. Every Sunday, schedule study hours just like your boss schedules your work hours. Show up for your academic job as religiously as you show up for work. This type of an approach is impressive and will help you manage a challenging situation.

Another proven method is to religiously track your assignments, meetings, tests, and other time constraints in an academic calendar or planner. This should be the one and only place you track your commitments. It doesn't have to be a fancy genuine leatherette number, just something that you can carry with you consistently to record assignments as soon as you learn of them. This habit greatly reduces the chance of missing a deadline, or needing to stay up all night to meet one. Like it or not, a planner will be part of your life after graduation. You might as well enjoy the benefits of using one on a regular basis while you're still in school.

Time management is a topic generally ignored by college students, but it is a valuable skill. Taking an evening seminar on time management or reading one of the many books on the subject is an excellent idea.

Classwork provides other organizational opportunities. A group assignment involving even a half dozen students needs an organizer to keep things on track. It's not a glamour job, but it can make a huge impact on the success of the project and helps to build a very important skill.

Extracurricular activities offer prime opportunities to get organized. As membership chairman of the chemical engineering society, for example, you'll need to develop or refine the membership tracking system, coordinate your efforts with other officers, and maintain files that your successor will need to be able to understand. All of these requirements help you build a Winning Characteristic and build your resumé at the same time.

Show What You Can Do

In interviews you may not field any questions aimed specifically at your organizational skills, but your answers to other questions will give clear clues of your ability to juggle priorities and get things done. Make sure you talk about your successes in organization even if that specific question is not asked. And remember that talk is cheap—you can't cover this base by simply claiming that you're efficient, timely, and organized. You need to prove it by citing specific examples of how you managed a variety of tasks simultaneously or brought order to a tangle of information.

Even the way you conduct yourself in the interview will send messages about your organizational skills. As the interview closes, ask when you'll be contacted about your status in the hiring process and record the date in your planner. And make sure you send a thank you e-mail or letter as soon as possible after the interview to demonstrate you're on top of your job search.

Organization may not be the most fascinating skill you'll ever develop, but it's definitely one of the most valuable. The sooner you get started the better.

Analysis

Where could you benefit from better organizational skills in your current classes, clubs, or jobs?

_____

_____

_____

_____

_____

Leadership

Leadership is not a title. It is not a position. Leadership is action. It is a philosophy—a way of making things happen that wouldn't happen without you.

Leadership is one of the key qualities employers desire in potential employees. Not every job is a true "leadership position," of course, but the leadership skill set is extremely desirable nonetheless. Even entry-level jobs will require taking charge of certain projects, and a manager will expect all employees to act as leaders as situations call for it.

Making Things Happen

"Making things happen that wouldn't happen without you." This simple phrase is a great starting point for understanding what leadership is all about, why it is so important, and how to demonstrate your abilities in this area in the recruiting process. There are many characteristics that combine to make a successful leader.

They include:

Courage—To lead, you must accept the risk of failure; you must make decisions and take action in the face of uncertain outcomes. Leadership requires a desire to succeed and willingness to risk frustration or failure, both for yourself and your team.

Vision—To be a successful leader, you need to see where a team needs to go and develop a plan to get there. You must be involved enough to understand an organization's problems and opportunities. Yet you must realize that you cannot do all the work yourself.

Motivational Skills—You need to make believers of the people around you, to gain their commitment to the common objective. This is not a one-time rallying cry, but continuous energy for achieving the goal. Motivation is both informational—helping others understand the goal—and emotional—helping them understand what's in it for them.

Persistence—Few goals are achieved on the first try and according to the pre-designed plan. A leader must adapt to conditions as they arise and continue to fight even when the road grows bumpy.

Leaders Are Not Appointed

We sometimes think of leaders as being appointed or elected. In truth, a leader cannot be appointed; we can only give people titles. Whether these appointed or elected people actually lead is not determined by their titles, but by their actions. Some club officers are effective administrators, but not leaders. Many so-called managers are totally inept at leading others, regardless of the titles they hold. In cases like these, others generally take informal leadership roles and exert more influence over the progress of the group than their "official" leaders.

Leadership skills clearly do not automatically accompany titles. Leadership skills, like any other skills, are developed through intentional effort, practice, and experience. Aptitude in this important Winning Characteristic can definitely be developed and refined.

Don't put yourself into leadership positions just for the sake of being in leadership positions. If someone tells me that he or she was the president of an organization, that alone isn't impressive. I want to know about the contributions you made to the group. Tell me how you left it a better place. If they had the role but didn't leave the group in better shape than it was in when they got there, that tells me something too.

Jeannie Maibe
Director of Management Consulting Recruiting
PricewaterhouseCoopers

Putting a Value on Leadership

Leadership is one of the classic intangibles—you can't put a dollar value on its importance. On the other hand, the cost of not having leaders is huge. A company, department, or committee that lacks leadership cannot consistently meet its objectives. As good as products or services may be, people are the fuel that make a company's

engine go. If a company has 10,000 employees—good employees—but they all put their heads down and wander without leadership, that company will never find lasting success.

> *If I had to choose one or two single most important things I look for in candidates, they would be intellectual capacity and leadership. We need to hire people that can work in complex global environments where problem-solving challenges abound—so raw capacity is critical. We also need people who can lead through the power of ideas. People who can demonstrate a pattern of setting a vision for change, energize others to support the effort, and enable them to succeed are the ones who consistently do well at P&G. Certainly we value team-based efforts, but the motto, "The power of one, the value of all" applies—after all, every team has a leader.*

> *Bill Reina*
> *Director, U.S. Recruiting, Training & Development*
> *Procter & Gamble*

Leaders are perhaps more valuable today than ever before. The marketplace demonstrates this in one respect by paying top executives many millions of dollars each year. But leaders at all levels, even entirely unofficial leaders, are highly valuable. One reason is the "flat" organization. Today there are fewer layers of management in most companies than there were 10 or 20 years ago. As management scientist and consultant Edward Deming's philosophy of total quality management swept the nation in the 80s and 90s, employees were given a greater say in the work process and entire levels of management were eliminated. The popular term for this concept has been "employee empowerment."

Employee empowerment has had mixed results, but one result is clear: the people who are most effective in this environment are leaders—people who can "make things happen," regardless of their job titles. It has created an opportunity for true leaders to step forward and make a real difference. Another important impact has been in recruiting; firms now more consciously seek those people who show the ability to take charge, risk failure, and drive great results.

Practice Leads to Leadership

During your college career, you can build real leadership skills and experience in many ways. The most obvious way may be to seek an officer position in a club, society, or other group. But don't confuse the title with the skill. Even if you are simply a member of such an organization, you can still play a leadership role by running a fundraiser, special event, or other project. Often by taking a non official guiding role, you will be identified as a leader and will be elected to an officer position in the next round of elections. Unofficial leadership roles provide a great opportunity to "get your feet wet."

You can also gain leadership practice by taking charge of a group project for a class, or by taking extra responsibility in a part-time job. In any case the key is "making things happen that wouldn't happen without you." Your impact on a club or project is much more important than simply showing up for meetings or earning a title for your resumé.

This same concept applies in an interview situation. You need to demonstrate how an organization was better, bigger, more efficient, more financially successful, recognized for achievement, etc., because of your involvement, your personal impact. Talking about real results like this is so much more powerful than just saying you were assistant treasurer of the Fishing Club or chairman of your campus Rubber Ducky Racing committee.

You can build a very impressive list of leadership stories during your college years. And it's worth the effort since these success stories will be among your most powerful tools in finding the job of your choice.

Analysis

Are there any groups where you hold a title but have not effectively "made things happen" that wouldn't have happened without you? What could you make happen in those roles?

_____

_____

_____

_____

_____

Logic

Logic, reason, intellect, brainpower, smarts. Whatever you call it, the ability to think, learn, and apply what you already know to achieve a desired result is one of the priceless skill sets all employers seek.

Nothing happens in business, whether it be in a manufacturing, banking, retail or travel firm, without employees making decisions. Of the many kinds of decisions made in every business, most fall into one of these categories:

Strategic decisions—What to sell, where to sell, what brand image to present to the public? These high-level choices guide the efforts of every person in the business—both what they do and how they do it. Strategy requires a clear view of the big picture and a realistic view of a firm's (or department's or team's) strengths and weaknesses.

Analytical decisions—What can be learned from data about the company, products, consumers, competitors, and other key variables? Is it more advantageous to make a product or buy it from a supplier? How should prices be set to maximize profits? To which customers should products be targeted? These choices often require proficiency with numbers, but, more importantly, require an understanding of the many variables that must be considered in even a seemingly minor decision.

Creative decisions—How can available resources be used to achieve a goal or solve a problem? This may involve traditional creative issues such as how to advertise a new product. Or creative thinking may be aimed at something as unglamorous as how to get a copy of a million dollar proposal to a customer in Europe when the printer is spitting out hieroglyphics and the cutoff for FedEx is in ten minutes. These decisions benefit from imagination, an open mind, and often the ability to blend the best parts of several possibilities to find the optimal answer.

Finding Point B

Whatever the specific type of decision, logic can be thought of as using your brain to get from point A to point B no matter what obstacles are in the way. Solving problems is what business success is all about—the companies that are best at recognizing and solving problems are most likely to survive and thrive. Because every business is at point A in some respect, every organization needs people who can help find the fastest, least expensive route to point B.

Consider this not-so-uncommon business problem. You work at Disk Connect, a software packaging company. You're the new kid on the block, but are finding some success. You have great package designers, superb technology, and reasonable prices. Your customers rave about your service. Unfortunately, you lack the marketing budget of your local rival, Digital Woo, so you're having trouble attracting new clients. Digital Woo has been around for almost a decade, has a more established clientele, and runs great ads in all the local business-oriented publications. These ads generate plenty of business. Disk Connect can't match that advertising; you need another way to attract new customers.

So what's the answer? Because generating new business is so important, you'll surely be a hero if you can find a way to reach your target audience without spending heavily on advertising. Sometimes the most important step in solving a problem is simply looking at the problem from a different angle. If you frame this problem as not about advertising but about sharing information, you may find new options. You suggest forming cooperative agreements with related companies, sharing referrals and contacts. You suggest a series of press releases about issues in the software industry that build the public credibility of Disk Connect. You suggest sending samples of your work directly to prime prospects instead of trying to match Digital Woo's mass advertising. You suggest a creative Internet advertising approach.

All of these ideas, whether they turn out to be the final solution or not, demonstrate your ability to find point B. This kind of thinking ability will be valuable in every kind of business, regardless of industry. It all goes back to the career commonalities discussed earlier in this book—every job involves solving problems and satisfying customers. That's why logic is one of the irreplaceable Winning Characteristics sought by recruiters.

You may think that entry-level jobs are mostly grunt work and involve very little problem-solving. After all, what do you know about solving complex business problems? This may be valid to some extent—you probably will not be hired into a job where you make important strategic decisions all day long. But you may be surprised how often you will have the opportunity to contribute ideas to a meaningful business issue.

Oddly, one of your best qualifications for solving problems may actually be your lack of experience. Doing it the same old way is a huge problem in many firms. You may be able to see options the "seasoned veterans" never would. You might not even know what the same old way is, so your answers will not be limited by the existing constraints. You also have the benefit of fresh knowledge, the latest academic theories, and the natural curiosity and imagination of a new graduate. These are better qualifications than you might realize.

No Answer Key

There are several major differences between solving problems in school and on the job. First, in business there is no "answer key" for the tests you'll face in the real world. A professor generally knows the answer before asking a question; your boss will ask you a question that needs a real solution that can be implemented. There's nothing theoretical about finding a way to cut medical insurance expenses.

This leads to a second major difference: accountability. If you make a wild guess on a test question, at most you lose 5–10 points, or then again you may get the answer right just by accident. In business, the consequences of your thinking and problem-solving skills are much more tangible. Great solutions can be your ticket to advancement. On the other hand, a terrible solution (or worse, a pattern of terrible solutions) may earn you disappointed looks from your boss, the least important or most boring assignments, or even probation or dismissal. Finally, business problems often have more than one right answer, making the decision process even more complicated.

Depending on the type and size of the firm you are joining, you may go through a training period where you attend classes or are supervised very closely.

But eventually you will be turned loose on a wide range of situations that require logical thinking and problem-solving. The largest national companies tend to have the most elaborate and lengthiest training. Smaller firms rarely offer this luxury, meaning the more knowledge and thinking skills you bring to the interview table, the better.

Making the Grade

So if thinking skills are so important, how can you demonstrate them to a recruiter? Unfortunately, many interviewers take a big shortcut in this regard by simply checking your resumé for your GPA. Grades are not necessarily a great predictor of post-graduation success, but they're an easy way to weed people out. If you didn't have either the thinking skills or the commitment to achieve decent grades in college, why should a recruiter believe you'll do better after college?

Think of an on-campus recruiter who returns to headquarters and tells the Director of Recruiting that he's picked a great candidate from State U. The student is very personable, energetic, and has a 2.1 GPA. Eyebrows go up. A low GPA makes it much more difficult for a recruiter to select you. Even a 2.9 will keep you in the running more often than a 2.1. And a high GPA can help a lot.

Now you surely know one or more 4.0 students who have no interpersonal skills or leadership abilities. These students may look great on paper, but in an interview may come up empty in other ways. Clearly GPA is not all that matters, but it does matter.

There are a number of ways students can prove to us that they possess strong analytical skills. First, they could give us some examples of how they think they are analytical and what their impression of their analytical skills is. For some, these examples might include course work—a class or classes in which they excelled. Statistics would be a good example of this kind of course material. We would also be interested in hearing about any problem that they have solved, regardless of whether it was work- or school-related.

Chuck Davis
Keane, Inc.

Real Solutions

Going beyond academics, there are many ways you can demonstrate your thinking skills to an interviewer. By presenting concrete stories about how you solved strategic, analytical, or creative problems, you can prop up a lower GPA or add an exclamation mark to a higher one. These stories need not be about how you launched your own space mission to Mars. The situations can be simple as long as they demonstrate how you personally made a difference using your thinking skills.

For instance, perhaps you are suffering in a dead-end job to help cover your college expenses. What suggestion could you make that would improve that business? Can you help the restaurant where you work to speed up the order-processing time so that they can turn tables more quickly? Or can you help the auto shop cut inventory by tracking parts by computer? Or can you help the computer repair center diagnose hardware problems more systematically?

In an interview, take every opportunity that arises to describe how you contributed new solutions to old problems, how you dug for the information you needed, analyzed it, and found new options. This is not about bragging or painting yourself as a hero, but about sharing how you helped to find a smarter solution. The interviewer will draw the appropriate inference.

Another way to demonstrate your intellectual ability is to discuss an important issue in your major, or a problem facing the interviewer's industry. This can happen at a recruiting reception, in an interview, or at a dinner with a recruiter who is hosting you for a second interview at corporate headquarters.

Analysis

What are the biggest challenges you're facing today (in and out of the classroom)?
Have you truly thought through how you'll solve them? If so, could they be utilized
in an interview situation? List the biggest challenges you're facing (and a few
you've recently managed effectively) in the space below.

_____

_____

_____

_____

_____

Effort

When the going gets tough, employers need people they can rely on to rise to the challenge.

"Give 110% effort every day!" It's an old cliché, but making an exceptional effort day after day definitely helps you stay on the list of most valuable players, in sports and in the world of work. Whether you call it motivation, commitment, or dedication, the willingness to do what it takes to get a job done is invaluable in every line of work, from landscaping to law enforcement. Employers want people who are willing to not only work hard, but in some cases to make personal sacrifices to make sure that deadlines and other objectives are met.

Getting the Job Done, and More

Employers know that a job is both a marathon and a sprint. They want individuals who can stay focused and perform consistently for the organization over an extended period of time and meet critical short-term deadlines as they arise. They want top performers in every job, every day of the week.

There's a big difference between having great potential and fulfilling that potential. The smartest candidate for a job may come up short against a candidate with average grades who consistently demonstrates extra effort, initiative, and a willingness to dive headfirst into a tough problem. As you advance in your career you will see this over and over—people of seemingly average skills who earn great responsibility on the best projects. These are the effort people.

Entry-level jobs are notorious for requiring a great amount of effort. It is often assumed that someone right out of college has unlimited capacity and energy. You will likely face high expectations from your employer. Your job may require early morning conference calls, extra travel, weekend hours, and more. The pace of activity may be extremely brisk all day long, and most workdays will not end when the clock strikes 5. An hour for lunch will likely be the exception to the rule, the rule being a bad sandwich wolfed down at your desk in nine-and-a-half minutes. Many first jobs are clearly not for the weak of heart.

In our business, it is absolutely critical that the individuals we hire be flexible and open to learn new things. If they wish to get ahead in our company, they must be willing to tackle new ground and try new things.

Allan Jones
Manager, College Recruiting
American Management Systems, Inc.

Are You Ready?

It's not a crime to be unwilling to make great personal sacrifices for the sake of your employer. In fact, it's a good idea to make a quick personal assessment of your effort level before you enter the job market. If the idea of working 50 or 60 hours a week makes you dizzy, you'll do well to stay out of jobs where those hours are typical.

Give the following questions some honest thought:

- Are you someone who typically does as little as possible to "get by?"
- Are you willing to do things that are not in your job description?
- Would you do some of your boss's work without getting special recognition for doing it?
- Would you do work that seems "below you" to keep a project on track?
- When you make a special effort, do you feel like a hero, a martyr, or just a hard worker?
- How much overtime would you work for free?
- Would you cancel or delay an evening with friends to finish a rush project?
- Is "getting ahead" important to you?
- Are you usually the first person to volunteer for a project, or the last?
- When you have free time, do you look for constructive ways to spend it, or do you head for the TV?

The answers to these questions may reveal your true rating in the area of effort. Since some jobs truly do require extensive effort, it's not hard to get in over your head.

On the other hand, for the ambitious, a high level of effort can be a great equalizer, both in the job market and on the job. If your qualifications are mediocre but you can show that you will do anything you can to make a project successful, you may get the nod over someone who has exceptional credentials and a couch-potato mentality.

Maximizing Your Efforts on Interview Day

A can-do attitude is definitely one of the most attractive qualities in a recruiter's eyes. But recruiters face a tough task in evaluating someone's effort level in the interview environment. Almost every job candidate will say something like: "I'm very conscientious and hard working." Very few, even the slackest slacker, will admit to laziness or lack of commitment. So if everyone claims to work hard, how can the interviewer distinguish the top performers in this area?

You can actually make it very easy for the recruiter. As you answer questions about the work you have done in extracurricular organizations and in internships and other work experience, be sure to identify those occasions where you went the extra mile. There's no need to brag about your heroics, but do describe in a positive way how you were so committed to the success of the project that you ended up doing more than was expected. Several stories like these will indicate your natural tendency toward achievement. Any quantifiable evidence will shine even brighter—if you beat your objective on a project by a wide margin, make it part of your resumé and interview arsenal.

"What is the most difficult situation you have ever faced, and how did you work through it?" This is a fairly standard interview question, and it provides a good opportunity to illustrate your level of motivation. The best answer will include concrete examples of how you did more expected of you. In other words, don't dwell merely on how you worked hard to get done what was expected; clearly explain that you made the conscious decision to do more. As always, if you have really given 110% in college, there will be no need or temptation to exaggerate your experiences—the truth will be very compelling to a recruiter.

Another common question offers a similar opportunity to sell your effort: "Tell me about a time in your college career when you had too much going on—between classes, work, outside activities—and you didn't think you could get it all done. How did you manage it successfully?" Not everyone can answer that question effectively. In fact, most students can't. If you can, you'll set yourself apart from the pack.

Make the Effort

So how do you develop these success stories? The best news on the subject of effort is that there are no limits. Your IQ may limit how much you can absorb on a particular subject, but your effort is purely a matter of choice. If you want to be the most dedicated member of a team or club, there's nothing preventing it. The first step is to get involved-you'll never be an overachiever on the Campus Activities Council if you never join the group. Once you get involved simply make yourself available for projects, put in a solid effort every time, and take the initiative to do more when needed. You'll gain credibility as a legitimate contributor, be seen as a valued team member by your peers, and ultimately earn roles of increasing responsibility.

Employers hire people who are willing to take the initiative to make things happen, so having a long college career of doing exactly that is great preparation for the job market.

I like to know how people learn new things on their own. Therefore, I like to ask questions related to this during the interview process. Specifically, I like to see how they will take initiative on the job and in the training. Oftentimes, there will be people who want training, want to learn, want to grow and do well with the company, but they won't take it on themselves to go out and learn as aggressively as we would like. Instead, they will wait for a manager to tell them it's time to learn or point them in the right direction.

I would rather know ahead of time whether someone has done it already and has taken the initiative to go out on their own and learn something new. In the answers, I'd like to know how quickly they can answer the question. What I find is those people who quickly reply by saying "well, I bought a computer a year ago and now I'm learning HTML at home" or "I recently bought a book on how to build a sailboat" or whatever it might be, generally possess some degree of self-initiative. This will help them grow in our company, and it will allow us to hire someone who wants to learn and that we don't have to push.

Chuck Davis
Keane, Inc.

Analysis

Based on your college record thus far, could you effectively convince someone that you're highly motivated? What two or three behaviors could you modify to increase your odds of success in doing so?

_____

_____

_____

Group Skills

The concept of "group skills" is fairly straightforward. To be successful, you need to be able to work effectively on a team. The concept is simple, but the dynamics of a group can be anything but. That's why employers look for people who can prove that they consistently work well in a wide range of group settings.

The ability to get along and work well with others—individually and in groups—is critical to career success, regardless of the field a student chooses to enter.

Dr. Robert Greenberg
Director, Career Services
University of Tennessee-Knoxville

Team Trends

Working together with others has been a fundamental component of completing large-scale projects since the dawn of civilization. It still is today. In fact the 1990s could easily be called the Decade of the Team. Virtually everything you do in your job will revolve around a team of some sort. In some businesses, teams are the central unit of organization. In other cases, your team could be a special project taskforce, a temporary group formed to solve a specific problem. In other cases, teams are less formal, just groups of people working together on a common project, objective, or customer need. What they are called doesn't really matter; the skills required are the same.

Many teams are interdisciplinary—composed of a variety of people from different functional areas (e. g., manufacturing, purchasing, sales, product development, etc.). Interdisciplinary teams are often employed to launch new products, taking an idea from the concept stage to rollout in the marketplace. For instance, a team might be brought together to design, optimize, produce, market, and sell a new telecommunications service in as short a timeframe as possible.

The concepts of "consensus building" and "self-directed" work teams have taken hold in the marketplace and appear to be here for good. With consensus building, the team doesn't move forward until everyone on the team is in agreement. It can be a slow process, but typically leads to good decisions. With self-directed work teams, groups take responsibility for their own success and enjoy limited supervisory involvement in their efforts. This arrangement has been found to be a strong motivator, and has led to many great successes.

Teams Make Great Things Happen

Teams do not just automatically run smoothly. You have probably been involved in some sports teams or other groups that worked particularly well together and others that struggled to accomplish anything. Poor-performing teams are often hindered by clashes of personality, ego problems, and other idiosyncrasies of human behavior. But many teams achieve great results despite the strong personalities of their members. Mutual respect and consideration are very important for success on any team.

Consider the team effort involved in the successful launch of Microsoft's on-line travel agency, Expedia. A project such as this required people with a very wide range of expertise, from travel to marketing to Internet programming to e-commerce to you name it. None of the people involved could have created Expedia individually. Not even half the team working together could have achieved the goal. It required the diverse expertise of all the different functional areas. Likewise, any member of the team who refused to cooperate, share information, or compromise with other members could have quickly derailed or delayed the project.

Honing Team Skills

Employers will seek to hire people who can work in a fluid team environment. They will look for individuals who demonstrate flexibility, reliability, tact, and a cooperative spirit. Do not confuse these traits with others like passivity or submissiveness. Teams need strong people who are ready to express and defend their ideas, as long as there is room for compromise and cooperation as well.

In many ways, being a student is a solitary existence. You pick your own classes, take your own tests, and rise or fall on your own skills, actions, and initiative. Your GPA, for instance, is yours alone. For that reason, making the transition to a team-based work environment is difficult for many new graduates.

Even if you're going to be a programmer and spend a lot of time working alone, you're still going to spend a lot of time working in tandem with other programmers. It seems as though the image of a programmer is that of someone sitting in a dark room staring at a computer screen, but that isn't necessarily the case anymore. There are so many collaborative efforts going on in developing programs.

Anne Gordon
Skills 2000 Program Marketing Manager
Microsoft

On the other hand, there are many great opportunities to learn and refine group skills while on campus. The classroom is an excellent place to begin to sharpen these skills. Group projects share many similarities with teams found in the work setting—each person brings different skills and interests to the group and all work toward a common goal. Eventually group projects will put you in a situation where you have a co-worker with whom you don't naturally "mesh with." The extra efforts you make to improve the relationship for the benefit of the team will be valuable experience and will make a good story to relate in interviews.

Keep in mind that every team is different, and your role will naturally vary because of that. If you find that you are always the designated leader of every group, you may want to take a less forward role in the next project. This flexibility will be valued by employers, and again, it makes a good story to share with recruiters.

Clubs offer other great chances to develop and enhance group skills. Bigger, more established organizations will be most helpful in this area, requiring interaction with a wider variety of people, and addressing more complex issues. For instance, you're more likely to improve your group skills on a committee composed of students, administrators, and faculty that deals with campus safety than simply being a member of the rugby club.

Nontraditional extracurricular activities should also be considered. A local chapter of the American Heart Association is one option. You'll work with diverse people of different ages, backgrounds, and experiences. Sure, it's tougher than working with a bunch of other 20-year-old students with similar backgrounds, ideals, and goals, but that's what provides the learning experience. This point will not be missed by recruiters.

One point to remember regarding clubs and activities: never join an organization just so it will appear on your resumé. Pick the clubs or causes that genuinely interest you. Your efforts will be much greater, and superior results will follow.

Answers and Questions

In an interview, count on being asked about teams you were a part of that you did not lead. Here are some of the key points you'll want to hit in your answers:

- How effective the team was at meeting its established goals
- What the ultimate result was—a grade, funds raised for charity, or other success
- What the biggest hurdle or conflict was and what role you played in resolving it
- What your most important learning was from involvement with a team that failed

These answers will be easy to develop if you have made a true commitment to a team. A lack of team experience and skills will be obvious if you can't give meaningful answers to questions like these.

Analysis

Think about the most and least successful teams of which you've been a part. What were the three biggest differences between the two teams?

1. _____

2. _____

3. _____

Entrepreneurship

The trusty dictionary describes entrepreneurship as organizing, managing, and undertaking all the risks of a business.

There's nothing new about this idea; millions of businesses around the globe have been started with the ideas and efforts of a single individual. Becoming an entrepreneur has become somewhat more common in recent years. The idea of working for oneself is highly appealing to many people—particularly after extensive experience in a field. Some large companies have contributed to the growth of entrepreneurship by continuing to pare down their workforces. This has given many very capable people additional incentive to start their own firms.

The entrepreneur is such an important part of the economy these days that many colleges now offer classes on entrepreneurship—covering what entrepreneurs do, how they succeed, and how to become one.

The entrepreneur is definitely "in fashion," and the term is being used not only to describe people who start and run their own businesses, but also those who bring the adventurous entrepreneurial spirit to tasks within larger organizations. It is this spirit that many employers will seek as they bring new people into a company. They are not necessarily looking for people who want to start and run their own businesses, but for those who will act like entrepreneurs in their areas of expertise.

What Makes an Entrepreneur?

The entrepreneurial qualities recruiters admire specifically include imagination, aggressiveness, an appetite for risk, high expectations, and persistence. These qualities can be very valuable when applied to running not only an entire business but also to small or large projects. An individual's willingness to embrace change, take initiative in an uncertain environment, and accept risks in exchange for potential rewards is very attractive to many companies.

Consider the situation of a hotel chain that is expanding—bringing on sixteen additional locations over a one-year period. The company will want experienced employees from inside the organization involved in the expansion, but may also seek new hires as well. The recruiters filling these spots will look for people able to work in a fast-paced, dynamic environment where the rules and procedures are being developed on the fly. The most attractive candidates will enjoy the uncertainty and frequent changes in direction inherent in the project rather than finding the process stressful.

In the interview process, demonstrating entrepreneurship means more than saying "Sure, I'm up for anything." Recruiters will want to see tangible examples of risk-taking and the other elements of entrepreneurship. If you have run your own business, whether it be a lawnmowing service or computer consulting business, you're well prepared. You'll only need to think of the challenges that best tested your entrepreneurial abilities and describe how you handled those challenges.

We like to see entrepreneurial experience on students' resumés. If they've actually developed their own small business—whether it's painting houses, mowing lawns, or providing some kind of service—this tells us a lot about that individual. In order to build a business, they've had to communicate well. They've had to figure out how they were going to say what they needed to say in a way that people would decide to do business with them.

Michael VanGrinsven
Associate Director of Recruitment & Campus Development
Northwestern Mutual Life Insurance

Getting Started

If you have not run your own business, you have two choices: start a business, or look for entrepreneurial opportunities in existing organizations. One could fill an entire book on business opportunities on campus, from bike repair to room decorating to word processing to tutoring to selling spring break vacation packages to creating an airport shuttle service at the end of every semester. The exact nature of the business is much less important than the risks you take, how you handle adversity, and what you learn from the experience. These enterprises make great additions to any resumé, especially when the description makes it clear that you started the business from the ground up. Be sure to list your job title as "owner," if it accurately applies.

Some new campus businesses require capital to get started; others require only effort and initiative. You should, of course, bite off only as much as you can chew. In fact, it may be possible to demonstrate your entrepreneurial abilities without even starting a business. Simply developing a solid business plan that describes what you would do if you had the money to get started will show an interviewer how your mind works. Even this "phantom" business would separate you from your less imaginative peers. Is a business plan easy to create? Of course not. But it may be worth the effort.

The other option is to find entrepreneurial experience elsewhere. For instance, successfully running a fundraising event for the Shakespearean Theater Club requires many of the attributes of an entrepreneur, including initiative and creativity. Many of the challenges you face in such a project would be great stories to share with an interviewer. Running any event on campus, in fact, would help you paint a picture of yourself as an entrepreneur in the making.

Or perhaps you are a member of a band. It may not seem it sometimes, but a band is a business. Even if you are playing for only $50 a night, the work involved in getting the group together, managing practices, marketing the group, and other essential activities definitely demonstrates entrepreneurial energy. Whether it's a band, a club, or a civic organization, look for the entrepreneurial opportunities in your life, wherever they may be. Showing through experience that you're prepared to take risks to get things done is powerful ammunition.

The importance of entrepreneurship may not get as much attention as that of communication skills or some of the other Winning Characteristics, but it is definitely a skill set valued in many businesses. And because many college students are weak in this area, it can be a great competitive advantage for those people who really live it.

Analysis

If taking risks often involves failure, why would large established companies be interested in it?

_____

_____

_____

_____

What is the most entrepreneurial thing you'll do this year? How can you stretch yourself in this area?

_____

_____

_____

_____

The Hidden E—Ethics

The first letters of the seven Winning Characteristics string together neatly to form the word COLLEGE. But there's one more letter, one more E, that's extremely important in the eyes of every employer. It's Ethics. Unlike the other Winning Characteristics, this is not a skill, but a way of thinking and acting.

Character Does Count

Honesty is an important character trait in all walks of life. Few worse things can be said of someone than "He can't be trusted." Once trust is lost in a person, one may doubt every word and question every motive. It jeopardizes friendships, breaks up marriages, and strains relationships of all kinds. In many cases it is almost impossible to re-establish trust after one or more dishonest acts.

Being caught in a lie in one's personal life can be very embarrassing and can ruin a treasured relationship. In business it can be devastating, as well. Trust is essential in business transactions of every type. If a product is advertised as hand-made, it had better be handmade. If an agreed upon price is later raised, a buyer may look elsewhere forever after. The consequences of lying, stealing customers, or sharing proprietary information can be far worse than embarrassing. They can cost people their reputations or their jobs, or lead to expensive lawsuits.

Character definitely matters to employers. There is nothing more frightening to a company than an individual who demonstrates all seven Winning Characteristics but lacks this hidden "E." A straight-A student who holds several positions of responsibility on campus, runs her own business during the summer, and volunteers at a hospital on weekends may seem like the dream employee of all time. But if that student is caught in a lie, even a minor exaggeration on her resumé, she will likely be crossed off the prospect list. Once a lie is discovered, it casts a shadow of doubt over all claims made on a resumé or in interviews. It's too risky to hire someone who is known to lie about material facts. In short, dishonesty can turn a promising job search into a direct path to the minimum wage.

> *During the interview process, students should make sure they are completely honest and that the level of integrity is there. Remember, an interviewer may know just as much, if not more, than a particular student about his university or the clubs on his resumé. Therefore, it is imperative that that individual doesn't try to embellish, hide, or misrepresent himself during the interview process. One of the things I've seen of late is someone claiming to be the president of an organization—but that organization includes two people, that person and his best friend. If you are a good interviewer, you are going to dig through that and come up with the truth. When that occurs, it certainly does not bode well for the conclusion of that interview.*

> *Peter Bowen*
> *General Electric Corporation*

The moral of the story is extremely obvious, yet it is ignored by many bright people: Don't cheat, lie, exaggerate, or in any other way mislead a potential employer. It is definitely not worth it. If your college record is not as strong as you'd like it to

be, there may be a temptation to "overinflate" a story or even to create one or two. Don't do it. The consequences simply aren't worth the risk. If you've ever seen someone caught cheating on a college exam, you have seen the painful downside of dishonesty in college. It creates a giant red mark that can't be easily removed from one's record (or reputation).

Prove Your Worth

Demonstrating your honesty to an interviewer is essentially impossible. The best you can do is to make sure that your resumé and everything you say in your interviews is completely accurate and unembellished. You can also make some choices that will cast your character in a positive light. Charitable and church activities suggest a high degree of moral character, for instance. A long history as a volunteer for the Leukemia Society or a similar organization says a lot of very positive things about you as a person. Don't miss the point here—don't join these groups to look honest, but real community service may increase your score in the ethics category.

Indeed, more and more employers are interested in hiring the type of people who give back to their communities. Every large company is involved in volunteer or charitable projects of some kind. It's a positive reflection both on the individual and the employer. Making it clear that you wish to participate in these charitable activities after you are hired can only help your chances.

> We definitely like to see members of our organization involved in community or civic-related projects. This preference is not limited to new hires, but applies to existing employees, as well. A lot of our people are active within the community on different advisory councils, groups, etc. . . . For example, I coordinate our School to Career Partnership

Programs with the high schools here in Colorado. And I'm on an advisory council at Red Rocks College.

> *Howard Roe*
> *Manager, University & Career Center Relations*
> *Lockheed Martin Astronautics*

Yes, this ethics discussion sounds pretty "parental," but it's an important part of finding and keeping the job you want.

Analysis

Is your current resumé 100% accurate in what it says and implies? If not, how will you need to modify it to achieve this objective?

_____

_____

_____

Are you currently involved in any organizations that "give back" to the community? If not, are there any that genuinely interest you?

_____

_____

Taking Personal Inventory

Where do you stand?

How do you stack up on each of these Winning Characteristics? You're probably encouraged that you've developed some of these skills already. Others you'd probably not even think about. That's fine—no one is born with all of the important skills preprogrammed into their beings.

The first step in assembling a complete, balanced set of skills is to understand where you are right now. So let's take a look at how you stack up on each of them. The goal in doing so is not to beat yourself up, but to give you a chance to honestly assess where you stand in the process and identify the areas where you need to focus your attention during the remainder of your college career.

What's Your Number?

The skill evaluation chart on the next page has spaces for two ratings for each skill. In the first, rate yourself on how effectively you've mastered the skill. A "1" means you need a lot of work and a "5" indicates you have fully mastered the skill. The second rating measures how effectively you could convince someone else that you possess this particular Winning Characteristic. You may be very proud of your leadership ability, but how will you prove it to a total stranger in the time crunch of an interview? Remember, the proof is in the story. Without great stories of how you exhibited the characteristic, you'll face an uphill battle.

The last column allows you to prioritize where you're going to focus your efforts between now and graduation (and into the beginning phases of your career). The key here is that you must change your behavior to change your results. If your communication skills are untested and undeveloped, for instance, you'll want to put new emphasis on that skill category. This rating process is a great way to set new priorities. Don't worry about the specific steps you'll need to take to build each Winning Characteristic—you'll explore those issues later in the book.

Personal Effectiveness Ratings

Winning Characteristic	Effectiveness (1–5 rating)	Ability to Prove (1–5 rating)	Priority to Improve (1–8 ranking)
Communication skills	_____	_____	_____
Organizational skills	_____	_____	_____
Leadership	_____	_____	_____
Logic	_____	_____	_____
Effort	_____	_____	_____
Group Skills	_____	_____	_____
Entrepreneurship	_____	_____	_____
Ethics	_____	_____	_____

1 = least effective
5 = most effective

The next section discusses how to make the most of academic, extracurricular, and work opportunities to build your personal skills. Following those chapters, you'll have a chance to make a personal plan to develop, practice, and document all eight of the Winning Characteristics.

SECTION 4

Advanced Strategies for the Home Stretch

Academics

What do you learn in college?

You learn facts—about historical events, scientific discoveries, and accounting practices. You learn theories—economic laws, investment strategies, the Big Bang. You learn skills—programming, writing, foreign language. You learn about the arts and artists—Hemingway, Monet, Bach. You learn a great deal about the world.

But more important, you also learn a lot about yourself through your education. You learn about what you value, how you want to spend your time, and what your strengths and weaknesses are. Some of this comes through specific classes, but much of it occurs simply by experiencing independence, getting to know a wide range of people, and being exposed to new and different ideas. Much of the education you receive could be covered in a class called You 101.

Learn to Learn

Finally, in college you learn how to learn. That's right, as odd as it may sound. When you start your career, even if you take a job closely aligned with your major, you'll find that your classes provide only the most superficial preparation for success on the job. Few businesses do anything "by the book." Most of what you will do on the job will be learned by watching, listening, and experimenting. The thinking skills you develop in college—problem solving, analysis, research—will be much more valuable to you than any single fact or theory you study. Simply learning how to efficiently find resources on the Internet, for example, will be valuable in almost any line of work.

The moral of the story is not to ignore or abandon your classes, even though many of them will not pay off directly on the job. The point is that you can greatly sharpen your critical-thinking skills by taking classes that genuinely test your abilities. The harder you work to solve a problem in your management or biology class, the better prepared you'll be to face the wide range of situations that arise in the workplace, even if none of them are remotely related to what you learned in class. Science has proven what has been presumed for decades: You can strengthen your mind simply by challenging and exercising it, just as you can strengthen your body through exercise.

Some Thoughts on GPA

Before exploring the role of academics in building Winning Characteristics, a couple of observations about the importance of grade point average in finding a job. First of all, grades matter. Second, other attributes matter at least as much.

Put your recruiter hat on for a moment. You have a stack of 100 student resumés on your desk. You have 16 interview slots. Eighty-four percent of the stack must be weeded out. You need a fast way to narrow the field. You apply a simple rule, fair or not: any resumé that lists a GPA below 3.0 goes in the discard pile. Immediately you've cut the field by about half. You've likely eliminated a bunch of people who would be great candidates. But you'll never know, because their grades are too low.

> *We start with a suggested minimum GPA of 3.0 but are not like some firms that will not interview a student if their GPA is below a certain level. We prefer higher grades than that but will sometimes hire a student with lower grades than that. What we really try to do is get behind the GPA and understand it. If a student's grades are a little lower than we would typically look for, we'll ask about it. We're looking for a reason. Students really need to understand the importance of their grades.*
>
> *Jeannie Maibe*
> *Director of Management Consulting Recruiting*
> *PricewaterhouseCoopers*

This method may sound quite arbitrary—it is—but it's not uncommon. Grades, for the most part, are used to weed people out rather than to select someone for a position. Maintaining solid above-average grades is worth the effort. A strong GPA in your major is a definite plus; it shows that you can apply yourself to what most interests you and that you're good at a field you're considering for your life's work.

So how hard, then, should you work to achieve a 4.0? Perhaps surprisingly, you'll probably open more doors for yourself by risking a B or two to get involved in other activities. If the choice is between a 3.5 with a solid list of achievements in clubs and some meaningful work experience, or a 4.0 with no activities, the former will often get the nod. The exception may be for students hoping for admission to top medical, business, and law schools, but not always; these institutions increasingly seek well-rounded candidates.

In short, remember that logic is only one of the Winning Characteristics. Don't forget the others while chasing the ever-elusive 4.0. If you have nothing more to talk about in interviews than your grades, expect to be very uncomfortable for 27 of the 30 minutes you spend with a recruiter. And if your grades are terrible and you're running out of semesters to bring up your GPA, realize that you have to improve your grades and work that much harder to build the other skills.

The Other Side of Academics

As alluded to earlier, the benefits of a strong academic experience hardly end with learning facts, theories, and specific skills. Your coursework also allows you to develop and demonstrate a number of the other Winning Characteristics. Let's look a little deeper.

Team projects in upper-level classes are a great opportunity to show many skills, group skills being the most obvious. Every group needs a leader, and you can definitely build your skills by taking a formal or informal leadership role on key projects. Keeping a study group for an education class on track can be more difficult than it sounds—just finding a schedule that works for all members can be a challenge. Acting as the leader often means that you'll present the results of your group to the class as a whole; you'll build organizational and communication skills in that role.

Some group projects, especially in business-related subjects, may even build some entrepreneurial experience. Many courses involve designing new products, solving complex case studies, or even running fictitious or real businesses. Whether the business is real or not, you'll learn some real lessons about entrepreneurship and build some powerful interview stories in such classes. A recruiter will be much more interested to hear how you wrote the business plan for a new business than how you wrote the thank you notes for the visiting speaker's club.

Investment classes more and more often involve managing imaginary portfolios (or you can do this on your own through numerous Web-based brokerages or on-line services). Working hard to maximize your investment return demonstrates both investment prowess and valuable dedication to a project.

Independent study classes are another great opportunity. For an independent study, you design the course, sell it to the professor, set the objectives, find the opportunity, and make it happen. It's an amazing chance available at many schools, but often ignored by students. Maybe a new architectural firm has opened in town. You might run its fledgling marketing effort for credit instead of money. Or perhaps you have a sincere interest in conservation or ecology, so you arrange to volunteer at a nature center, help with research there, and write a paper for your grade. Independent study opportunities are limited only by your imagination and your ability to convince/ persuade a professor or department head to back you. A word of advice: scout these classes out early and find out how to register for them; there are often special rules.

Show and Tell

And don't forget that an interview can include some show and tell. Major term papers or a thesis can be an excellent opportunity to showcase your work to a future employer, especially if the paper relates to the employer's industry or interests. You can take a copy of a paper to an interview, or list a Web link on your resumé. Or if you have an interactive on-line Wired Resumé, a link can be made directly from the resumé to examples of your work. It's unlikely that a recruiter would read your entire work, but just seeing your pride in your efforts and your willingness and ability to showcase it makes a positive statement.

In an interview, you've got to sell yourself today. Bring something you did personally—bring a project, an invention, something that shows initiative and innovation, and that you personally developed. Achievement in college shows that you are ready to take it to the next level and make a contribution to a company. Show me. Make it a show and tell experience.

John Zweig
Corporate Employment Manager
Apple Computer

We'll talk later about networking, but academics offer many excellent connections, especially with and through professors—some of whom can be outstanding allies in your career search.

In any case, look at academics through the widest possible lens. Classes provide the chance to build many skills beyond thinking, test taking, and crunching numbers. With a little creative thought, you can strengthen your job options considerably through academics, even if you make less than a 4.0.

Analysis

What are your current overall GPA and your GPA in your major? What are your goals for these two measures at the end of your junior year (you'll start interviewing at the beginning of senior year)? What level of performance will you need along the way to achieve these?

_____

_____

_____

_____

List three ways you can change your academic efforts to help you land the job of your choice.

_____

_____

_____

Extracurricular Activities

There's more to college than going to class. Lots more.

Sixteen hours per week. At most schools, that's the magic number of hours you need to spend in the classroom to graduate on time. Assume 8 hours per night for sleep and that leaves about 96 hours each week for everything else. Even if you're a diligent studier and work part- or full-time, you can definitely make time for involvement in clubs and activities if you're truly committed to doing so.

Extracurricular activities can be a very valuable and enjoyable use of your time. Committing just a few hours a week can make the difference. From a recruiter's point of view, involvement beyond academics is a major plus. And, the activities don't have to be anything you dread. They can and should be a lot of fun. The key is to choose organizations that match your interests, both academic and otherwise. If you hate foreign films, the Foreign Film Society will be a poor choice—you won't be interested or committed, you won't attend, and you won't achieve anything there. On the other hand, you can turn an interest in hang gliding into a very positive interview success story by leading or forming such a club.

With respect to extracurricular activities, I really stress that it's important to become active in various organizations. What type of organizations students join should depend on their individual interests and course of study. In order to maximize the experience, students should try to assume some leadership roles within those organizations.

Howard Roe
Manager, University & Career Center Relations
Lockheed Martin Astronautics

Join with a Strategy

You can find benefit from almost any club. The specific organization you join is much less important than what you do there. Because you only have so much time to devote to activities, develop a membership strategy. Instead of joining every club in sight, start with a couple related to your hobbies or interests. These can be anything from the concert board to the ski club to the campus chapter of a religious or political group. Then join one or two organizations related to your major or intended work field. Most majors have clubs that host speakers, discuss relevant issues, conduct research, or help to connect students with employers.

Clubs related to your major offer many benefits. First, they show that your interest in a subject extends beyond the classroom. They also provide a reliable source of information from the real world. You'll learn what recent graduates are experiencing in your field, where the opportunities may lie in the future, and how you can best prepare for your career. You may also gain valuable experience working on projects related to the subject area. Through these activities you may even meet someone who can help you find an internship or full-time position.

> *Think how hard it could be to answer a simple question like, "Tell me about a time in your life when you overcame a significant obstacle and how you did it." For most people a lot of possible examples will flash through their mind—some personal, some school-related, some family-, social-, church-, or sports-related. Which example is the strongest one? Which best demonstrates their capacity to get results in a difficult situation? Which one best represents the values and approaches that are most important to them? The student has only a few seconds to make up his or her mind.*

> *Bill Reina*
> *Director, U.S. Recruiting, Training & Development*
> *Procter & Gamble*

By joining the Marketing Club, Engineering Circle, or Future Teachers' Network, you gain access to a wide range of information. But joining is only the first step. You should look at clubs as a place to build and demonstrate key skills, including communication and leadership. Being a member of ten organizations says nothing about your abilities. Recruiters don't care whether you're good at joining—they want to know what you can do to help an organization achieve its goals. It's what you do after you join that matters.

This raises an interesting point: some honorary societies have no goals except to induct new members, distribute lapel pins bearing the club's logo, and collect checks to pay for the effort. These organizations offer few opportunities to prove yourself or refine your skills. It's no crime to join an honorary and buy a pin, but realize that it will likely have little impact on your job search success.

Work Your Way UP

When you've selected the right organizations for your interests and become a member, you begin a building process. Call it paying your dues or any other name, but basically you need to work your way up through the ranks in order to make a lasting impact on the organization. That's what employers really seek—people who can make things happen. Just realize that it is often impossible, and sometimes inadvisable, to try to do too much too soon in a club.

Consider the case of Jamie, a second-semester freshman who is a new member of the Journalism Society. Jamie wants to make the most of his involvement in the organization to improve his chances of landing a reporter position with a daily paper in a major market. The day after he joins he submits his name as a candidate for president of the society in an upcoming election. He sends every student in the membership a four-page letter describing how dedicated he is to the society and of all the plans he has for making it a better organization.

It will be no surprise to anyone but Jamie that he is not elected president. The members of the society may be impressed by his energy, but his aggressive reach for a leadership role will not be embraced by the members; some may even be offended. Instead, Jamie would be better off to *earn* the leadership role he seeks. He needs to build a series of small successes, working on society projects or committees with other members. Each small success and positive idea contributed makes Jamie a more attractive and appreciated member of the group and a more likely candidate for leadership.

All of these smaller successes also practice and build the fundamental skills that employers seek. Employers want people who can take a step back, understand the challenge at hand, devise a solution, and put it into place. Managing a speaker series for the Journalism Society, for example, provides plenty of opportunity to hone skills—managing a schedule, communicating with speakers, keeping members apprised of progress, soliciting and implementing ideas from others, etc.

So the story has a happy ending for Jamie if he starts small and works his way up. He has plenty of time to reach an officer position and implement the ideas he has in mind. That's an important point: join early. Waiting until spring of junior year to get involved in campus activities severely limits the impact one can make on the organization. Freshman year is a great time to scope out potential clubs, and joining no later than sophomore year is ideal.

If it seems there are no organizations on campus that interest you, here are three pieces of advice:

Look harder—even small schools are awash in organizations of every type.

Start your own—in what better way could you demonstrate effort and entrepreneurial spirit?

Look off campus—consider volunteer work in the local community or in your hometown during the summer.

In whatever organization you join, remember it is your contribution, not the club itself or the specific title you hold, that matters most. With this in mind, a few words about fraternities and sororities.

It's All Greek

Whether to join a Greek house or not is an absolutely personal decision, and one that should be made with as much information as possible. If your school offers this option and you choose to rush, learn as much as you can about a house before you make any commitments. That said, a fraternity or sorority can be an excellent place to build valuable skills for the job market.

Every Greek house needs many responsible and productive members to keep the place in good physical and financial standing. From treasurer to alumni director to house manager to special events chairperson, the opportunities to develop and demonstrate skills are considerable. Even in a large house, one dedicated member can have a huge impact on its success by tackling the difficult situations as they arise. As always, the key is to build a set of success stories that prove how the house was better because of your involvement.

You definitely should not join a Greek house (or any other organization) purely for its merit on your resumé, but if you choose to join a house, make the most of it. And like any other involvement, don't put all your eggs in one basket. A well-rounded set of activities based on your hobbies, major, and so on, is preferable to any single membership, no matter how prestigious it may seem.

One final place to look is with local charitable organizations. They are always understaffed and always looking for people to take on more responsibility. If you're an upperclassman and haven't been involved with any meaningful groups yet, charitable groups may represent a great opportunity—if you're legitimately interested. You can get involved and begin to take on responsibility quickly—making a major impact in a short amount of time (with a lot of hard work, of course).

Analysis

Looking forward, what organizations on campus will be the places where you'll have a meaningful, positive impact?

_____

_____

_____

Work Experience

For many students, meaningful work experience is now as fundamental to college success as going to class.

Over 45% of this year's seniors will have internship or co-op experience when they graduate. Gaining work experience before you graduate is no longer a luxury that sets you apart—it is now expected in many fields. In fact, some research studies indicate that work experience in the field is the number one hiring criteria for recruiters. Think about that—that's their top criteria for an entry-level position! When recruiters make work experience such a priority, it must become a priority for any student who's serious about landing a top-tier job.

Why Work Experience Works

Hiring firms have many good reasons for favoring experienced candidates. Your work experience demonstrates, among other things:

- Some record of success in a job similar to the one for which you're interviewing
- A practical, versus purely academic, understanding of job duties and industry issues
- The specific skills you've developed and applied to real-world situations

I think that outside work experience is really critical because working students have had to come up with creative solutions to solve problems. Therefore, I would rather see them working than not because it enables them to develop some good problem-solving skills.

Michael VanGrinsven
Associate Director of Recruitment & Campus Development
Northwestern Mutual Life Insurance

Work experience also allows a recruiter to talk to your internship boss or other co-workers about your performance and potential. And receiving an offer for full-time employment from the firm where you had your internship is further evidence of your abilities and value. Ultimately, many employers, even those recruiters with great educations, tend to trust work experience more than academic training for a job. So the more positive input they can find about your performance on the job, the more inclined they will be to hire you.

It makes sense—if you can say "I've done that" to every responsibility listed on a job description, you gain instant credibility, even if you've only earned a C or two in classes related to the subject matter.

I would encourage all students, prior to interviewing with our company, to secure an internship or co-op experience with us. In fact, the single best way to find out about our organization is to try us out for a period of time. This grants us the opportunity to look at prospective job candidates, as well.

I would hope that, in the very near future, 50% of all of our full-time hires will have had an opportunity to do a co-op with us.

Peter Bowen
General Electric Corporation

Check It Out

Meaningful work experience also has some very important personal benefits for you. Internships are invaluable test drives of your chosen field. You may love your law enforcement classes, but a semester as a clerk in a sheriff's office will give you a much clearer, more realistic look at the field. Or a co-op job with a software firm might teach you that your intended career as a programmer isn't as appealing as you originally thought and that you're better suited to selling or implementing systems.

No matter how much research you do about a particular field, you can't really evaluate it until you've lived it. Learning these lessons in the no-risk atmosphere of work-study saves you the strong possibility of seeking and accepting a job that's not right for you. Think of the number of people you know who have changed jobs in their first year or two of employment. It's a common, and often avoidable, situation.

We encourage students to consider internship experience early and to participate in several internships. Our university has two main offices that list internship opportunities and an internship career fair is also hosted. Credit internships should have clear learning objectives incorporated into them. Regular supervision should be provided as well as a job description. Students should also understand that the internship should be a learning experience. Expectations need to be discussed with the employer before agreeing to participate in the internship.

> *Anne Scholl*
> *Acting Director, Center for Career Services*
> *University of Washington*

Making the Most

Not every college work experience is a nice paying, high-visibility intern assignment with a Fortune 500 firm. You may end up working part-time in a repetitive, low-paying, mind-numbing job on or near campus to allow you to afford to be there. A student's financial facts of life often require grunt work like this at some point, but a positive, goal-oriented outlook on such work can lead to much more than just a weekly paycheck.

Most rotten jobs are hourly; you're paid to show up. The natural response in this kind of work is often to do as little as possible. "Put in the time and get out of there." It's a natural inclination, but not a great idea. A much better approach is to do as much as possible. Overachieve. Ask for additional responsibility. Ask to learn an additional skill on your own time. Offer to computerize records now stuffed in filing cabinets. Surprise your boss with the quality of your work and range of abilities. Someone has to be the top-rated part-time person in every company; only good things will happen to you if you are that high achiever.

Imagine going into an interview with 4 or 5 great letters of recommendation from boring "dead end" jobs. It will say a lot about who you are. If you were willing to work that hard in an unsatisfying, no-brain job, you'll look like pure potential for the "real" job the recruiter has to offer. And, since you typically get paid by the hour, the high-energy approach will cost you no more time than the "do as little as possible" strategy.

Success Stories

You can also fortify your arsenal of skills in a no-future campus job. Recall that interviewers are looking for clear demonstrations of the Winning Characteristics. An after-class secretarial job provides great opportunities to build organizational skills. Telemarketing jobs offer communication opportunities galore. Even being a shift manager at a fast-food restaurant demonstrates some level of leadership prowess. Remember, many interviewers have had lousy jobs early in their careers; showing how you made the most of your situation is always preferable to complaining about what the job lacked, or how it was beneath you.

Even in jobs that seem to place no importance on thinking, you can definitely exercise your logic skills. It's all about seeing a problem that limits efficiency, growth, or other key results, and devising a realistic solution, whether this problem is your responsibility or not. One thing is for sure—every business, large or small, has problems. Offering practical solutions can lead to better assignments, letters of recommendations, or even offers of full-time employment after graduation. Just remember that you were hired to do a specific job. That job must be your first priority—don't abandon your post to devise a solution to a problem in another part of the operation.

Some students work of necessity, to make sure the tuition check doesn't bounce. For those students lucky enough to have no money worries, work may be less urgent, but no less important to finding success in the job market. Every student, regardless of finances, should look at the work world as another essential part of the preparation for a successful career, just like academics and extracurricular activities.

And work experience during college need not be in the field you choose for your full-time career. Any work experience is better than none. Even the worst jobs on earth—cleaning the slaughterhouse, for example—will yield at least one great benefit: never wanting to work in that kind of job again! Terrible jobs can be great motivators.

Internship activity is one of the fastest growing components of a student's education today. Employers see it as a reasonable real-world work experience, as do students. Assumptions can be tested about interest and content of a given field all for relatively low risk. Even internships that were not so positive, offer those students more insight about what to avoid in the future. Many academic departments offer credit and some will have a collection of good internship potential depending on your major. Campus Career Centers will also catalog a multitude of opportunities as well as provide access to directories, web sites, and pos-

sible internship fairs. Many will be paid but some will not. Take care to understand your own expectations and the actual daily content of the work to be expected—especially if you are anticipating the granting of academic credit. Avoid those situations that sound like you will be treated as a source of cheap labor with little offered in return—no one wants to be taken advantage of.

Dr. Wayne Wallace
Director, Career Resource Center
University of Florida

Analysis

What is the worst job you've ever had? How could you have approached it differently to get more out of it? What insight does this give you for your current (or next) job?

_____

_____

_____

_____

_____

Your Personal Strategies

It's all a matter of choice.

The strategies discussed in the previous three chapters just plain work. Taken together, they form a map that can help you excel in all aspects of the college experience—in ways that you may not have considered. The first step, though, requires your personal commitment to follow this map to success. Building an indisputable record of accomplishment, the kind of resumé that will find its way to the top of every interviewer's priority list, takes considerable effort and attention. It simply comes down to a matter of choice.

This is your chance to make a personal plan to bring these success strategies to life. For you it may mean "business as usual," continuing to do the types of things you're already doing. The book has confirmed that you are heading in the right direction, building your skills through academic, extracurricular, and work experiences. You may wish to make some minor adjustments to maximize your effectiveness—but you're on the right track.

Or maybe you realize that you need to do more, perhaps much more, to build the skill set recruiters are looking for. You're doing well with some of the Winning Characteristics, but still have significant holes in your credentials. You need to step on the accelerator in one or more key areas.

Or maybe this is a major wake-up call for you. You realize that if you don't get your act together you'll end up with a job you could have gotten with a high school diploma. You now understand that without a significant change in strategy, you'll look back on college as a very expensive mistake.

Your Personal Plan

Regardless where you fall on the personal progress meter, now is an ideal time to chart a course for further improvement. If you set goals today, you'll be much more likely to find yourself where you want to be 3, 5, 10, or 20 years from now.

The area below is your chance to build your own personal improvement plan. The chart allows you to set specific goals for academic, extracurricular, and work experience goals that will ensure that by graduation your Winning Characteristics portfolio is full of success stories. Create specific 12-month goals for each area. These are important steps, so take the time to think through what you need to accomplish during the next year to keep you on track for great results after graduation. You may even want to start your goal list now and review it again in a day or two.

Make Them Count

When setting the goals, three characteristics are most important. Set your goals to be meaningful, manageable, and measurable.

Meaningful—they set a challenge you would not normally achieve. Setting easy goals that you can quickly check off as accomplished may create a sense of progress, but won't help you fulfill your longer-term expectations.

Manageable—they are realistic. You can't go from being a member of no clubs to being president of three in a six-month period. You need to set goals that are attainable—challenging, but not impossible.

Measurable—they are trackable. Set goals that are quantitative or created in some way that will allow you to know if you met your objective. A goal to "get more involved in extracurricular activities" is not nearly as measurable or as effective as a goal of "joining two more organizations related to my field of study and running a committee in each group."

Here are some examples of goals that don't meet the meaningful, manageable, and measurable criteria:

<u>Ineffective Goals</u>	<u>Better Alternatives</u>
• Be a better student	• Raise GPA in major to 3.4
• Go to all monthly Marketing Club meetings	• Join the Marketing Club; contribute to the Guest Speaker program
• Start a business	• Establish a tutoring service or PC training business

Your Turn

Now's your chance to make some commitments to yourself. When you've completed the exercise, cut out the page and post it somewhere where you'll see it on a regular basis. If you look at your goals regularly, you're more likely to do something about them.

Area	Goals	Start Date	Completed By

Academics:

Target GPA: _____

1. _____
2. _____
3. _____
4. _____

Extracurricular Activities

1. _____
2. _____
3. _____
4. _____

Work Experience

1. _____
2. _____
3. _____
4. _____

SECTION 5
Polishing the Apple

Selling Your Strengths

It happens all the time in business. A small company has a revolutionary new product, something that's genuinely better and different than anything else on the market. And it never sells because no one knows about it.

The same thing happens with many college students—they have great credentials but don't effectively demonstrate their potential to employers. In the ever-competitive job market, there's a simple rule of survival: Even if you've got the goods, you still need to prove your value to a potential employer to earn the job.

> *In the beginning, companies are selling and students are buying. Later on, students are buying and companies are selling. That's what the recruiting relationship is all about.*
>
> *Bill Reina*
> *Director, U.S. Recruiting, Training & Development*
> *Procter & Gamble*

Make the Sale

To land the best possible position, you need to be an effective salesperson, and the product is you. Selling any product can be difficult, and it's no easier when you are the product. To be an effective salesperson—of appliances, banner advertising, aluminum siding, or anything else—you need to understand the customer and what she values, and then prove to her that your product will most effectively deliver the results she seeks.

In the process of selling yourself to the organization of your choice, you have a distinct advantage. You've read this book, so you already know what the customer wants—it's the Winning Characteristics! You not only know what they are, you know how to build them and should have a plan in place to do so. If you don't, now would be a good time to go back and set your goals for the next year. (See Your Personal Strategies.)

A Long-Term Sale

If you expect the sale to take place in the interview, you're partially right. The interview is a tremendous opportunity to make your case, but the sale actually begins before the interview and ends well after it. Selling is part of every interaction with your potential employer.

Selling yourself begins when you first make contact with the people who can help you attain your desired job. Much of that effort falls in the category of networking (the subject of the next chapter). The next step is the development and refinement of your resumé and, in some cases, a cover letter. Only then does the interview process begin (for many jobs there may be several rounds of interviews involving a dozen or more people before a job offer is actually made).

Because so many students are competing for the best jobs, recruiters for these positions are often looking for ways to screen people out of the process. That means a poor showing in any of these sales steps may take you immediately out of the running. It is not unheard of for students with excellent credentials to be removed from consideration simply for a single grammatical mistake on a resumé. Without a doubt, you need to make your best efforts in all phases of the process.

Your Life on a Page

Let's look at the resumé. There are many books that deal exclusively with the content and look of your resumé. It is a good idea to review these books or use an on-line resumé resource. No matter how you develop your resumé, here are a number of fundamentals to remember.

Maybe most important to understand is what a resumé should not be. It should not be a chronological accounting of your college experience. It shouldn't simply list what groups you joined and what jobs you had in each school year. Many students miss the mark on this point, so doing it correctly will set you apart.

What a resumé can be when developed correctly is a personal showcase of your skills and experience—an informative, impressive, and persuasive document. First of all, before you even begin to write your resumé, get into the Winning Characteristics mindset. Think about each of your academic, extracurricular, and work experiences in terms of leadership, entrepreneurship, and the other key qualities employers look for. Be sure that you recognize the huge difference between activity and accomplishment. As you write your resumé, focus on the results you created, not just on how you spent your time. Make it as clear as possible how you stood out from your peers, how your contributions or efforts had a clear impact.

Take a minute to analyze two possible ways of communicating projects and/or jobs on a resumé. By the way, these are not just fictitious examples. The transformation of this resumé to better reflect this student's true accomplishments took this student from the frustrating situation of little interest in her on the part of major companies to an internship at Motorola and a full-time job with Procter & Gamble. The "after" resumé was still 100% accurate. It simply communicated her true role and accomplishments much more effectively.

Before

Pi Sigma Epsilon, business fraternity, 1995-Present
Chairperson for 1996 Regional Convention

After

Pi Sigma Epsilon, business fraternity, 1995-Present
Chairperson for 1996 Regional Convention
- Coordinated a three-day program for 125 students from six universities, including hotel accommodations, travel arrangements, and catered meals
- Arranged three educational speakers and a job fair consisting of eight national companies including Procter & Gamble, Andersen Consulting, and E&J Gallo Winery
- Obtained sponsorship donations from 10 companies
- Nominated for Top National Project Manager

Before

Dispatcher and Emergency Medical Technician, 1994 to Present
- L.E.A.D.S. Certification
- National Registry EMS Certification

After

Dispatcher and Emergency Medical Technician, 1994 to Present
- L.E.A.D.S. certified to access and transmit information about vehicle registration, driving records, warrants, and officer safety bulletins
- Trained to receive and dispatch 911 emergency calls
- National Registry EMS certified to respond to all emergency medical calls. Requirements for certification include 120 classroom hours, 12 hours of emergency room aide, and 24 hours of continuing education each year.

Before

Internship with Mercantile Co., Fairfield, Ohio
Department manager of women's sportswear, Summer of 1996
- Monthly sales plans
- Visual presentation of merchandise
- Experimental project—Gift Registry with personal shopper

After

Internship with Mercantile Co., Fairfield, Ohio
Department manager of women's sportswear, Summer of 1996
- Developed and successfully exceeded monthly sales plans

- Created visual displays for new merchandise in several locations throughout the store and tracked the number of sales to determine the most successful locations for generating impromptu sales
- Designed an experimental gift registry system allowing customers to complete a gift wish list with merchandise throughout the store. Gift purchasers could obtain the list at customer service at all times. Objective was to increase customer satisfaction, increase store loyalty, and reduce expenses incurred from merchandise returnees. Project included estimating expenses for implementation, maintenance, and promotion.

Resumé Quick Tips

- **Use action words**—like led, managed, sold—whenever possible. Let them know you DID something versus just held an office.
- **Make it dynamic**—use strong adjectives ("looking for a position in a dynamic, growth-oriented firm that will allow me to take on meaningful challenges and be rewarded for strong measurable results.") Remember, this is a sales document.
- **Talk results**—if you raised participation by 50%, secured a new corporate sponsor, or raised funding by 32%, say it. Recruiters like people who have a track record of delivering results.
- **Be specific**—have specific career objectives that match up to specific jobs. Don't just develop one generic resumé and use it everywhere.
- **Pick the length**—don't be afraid to go beyond one page *if* you have a lot to say. You need a one pager, but may want to develop a more detailed version for the office visit.
- **Proof your work**—this idea cannot be stressed enough. One dumb mistake may cost you a chance to prove yourself in an interview.

The same general idea applies to your cover letter—stress your accomplishments and impact, not just that you're "highly interested in employment with the XYZ Company."

To stand out, a student's resumé must be creative, innovative, and truly express what they're doing.

John Zweig
Corporate Employment Manager
Apple Computer

Keep Your Inventory Stocked

While this sounds more than obvious, part of being successful in this sales effort is remembering everything you accomplished in college. As you progress in the interview process, interviews often increase from as few as 20 minutes on campus up to an hour or more when you visit the company's offices. Producing an hour of succinct examples of how you've built and exhibited the Winning Characteristics can be difficult. Pulling the perfect example from your memory at a moment's notice can be just as challenging.

Be clear about skills and strengths and be able to articulate them; provide evidence for strengths.

Anne Scholl
Acting Director, Center for Career Services
University of Washington

Make it as easy on yourself as possible by writing down your accomplishments on a regular basis. Record the things you have done well and which of the Winning Characteristics they demonstrate. Many achievements will support more than one of the skills you hope to demonstrate.

Know your strengths, how they benefit an employer, and be ready to articulate them to employers.

Terri Gelles
Director, Career Center
Mount Saint Mary's College

At the end of this book you will find a section called the Winning Characteristics Tracker. Utilize it as a diary of your successes throughout the process. It only takes a minute or two to record a success, and it will help considerably as you write your final resumé or prepare for an interview. And don't forget your major high school accomplishments. Use the best of these to demonstrate your ongoing pattern of achievement and involvement.

At all times, remember that you're selling yourself. A high-quality product does not need exaggerated claims or trickery to generate sales, but it does require that potential buyers understand what the product can do. If you keep this in mind as you present yourself on paper and in person, you're sure to improve your prospects.

Analysis

Assuming you had to sell someone today on the fact that you are the perfect candidate for their organization, what would you tell them your top three assets are (remember the Winning Characteristics)?

_____

_____

_____

Building Your Personal Network

Networking can be a powerful tool if you choose to use it.

The core principle behind networking is that everyone you meet can be a possible source of information, contacts, or business. Believers in this philosophy take every available opportunity to "work the network," that is, to make contacts, share information, and use these relationships to achieve their objectives. Networking has evolved into a common and accepted practice in all aspects of business and government. If done properly, it is not sneaky, unethical, or in any way undesirable. You should make it a part of your career search process, and a permanent part of your career.

You may argue that what you know is more important than who you know. That sounds great, but the truth is that your success will rely on your ability to demonstrate the Winning Characteristics to people in a position to hire you. If your network allows you to better develop your list of success stories or to meet more people in a position to hire you, your chances of landing a prime job will obviously improve. Networking rarely results in an unqualified person getting a great job; it merely expands the opportunities for well-qualified candidates.

Some students may frown upon their peers whose parents "know all the right people." In reality, everybody knows someone, or can meet someone, who can help in the job search. By implementing ideas in Section 4 of this book (academics, extracurricular activities, work experience), you are certain to meet people who can exert a positive influence on your career search. Simply making the effort to get to know a professor or introducing yourself to a speaker at a program can help in your quest for a great job. Taking this initiative again and again only improves your chances further. Be clear on this point: there is definitely nothing unethical or wrong about developing well-connected contacts in the career search process.

Networking occurs at a multitude of levels emanating from every contact you have ever made in the classroom, with friends, fellow students, Campus Career Centers, past employers, as well as all the leads generated from social and occupational channels. It's true that only a small portion of the labor market engages in traditional campus recruitment activity and that those efforts are heavily focused toward engineering, technical, and business types of graduates.

Once one leaves the university environment, EVERY job you will ever have will come about because you somehow made a case about your candidacy. Even for those highly sought by employers, they will still be a party to some type of "network" system, whether it's a friend, professional association, reference, University Career Center, WWW, or former employer. It all counts, so it's a matter of your ability and interest in parlaying your assets to your advantage. Learn how to network effectively while on campus, while you are surrounded by all those friendly experts at the Career Center who are so willing to teach how to succeed for no cost at all, other than time and energy.

Dr. Wayne Wallace
Director, Career Resource Center
University of Florida

A Great Start

On a nuts and bolts level, networking means meeting people, making a positive impression, staying in touch, and sharing

information, ideas, and guidance. Networking is a give-and-take process where you will help others as much as you are helped.

Here's how networking might work for you. You're interested in a banking career. You're a member of the campus business (or investment or finance) club. An alumnus of your school, who has a job very similar to the one you seek, comes to talk to the group. After his speech you introduce yourself, talk for a while, and ask him if you might call him to discuss what he has learned since he graduated. He agrees. You get his business card. You send him an e-mail right away to remind him of the discussion. You call him a week or so later and ask him more about his job and what he would have done differently in school. (Most people love to answer sincere questions about themselves.) You keep in touch by e-mail and ask for some ideas on which banks would be the best employers. You ask if he knows anyone at those banks, or anyone else you might contact to gain more insights into the industry. Realize that you are not asking him for a job or an unfair advantage—just helpful hints, insights, and ideas.

At this point, the alum is part of your network, someone you can turn to for advice, and someone who will want to help you if he can. Meanwhile, you make yourself available to others in the club. Maybe you have a relative in the manufacturing field. You help a fellow student interested in robotics by connecting her with your manufacturing contact. If you do enough of this—building relationships and helping others build relationships—you will end up with a surprisingly long list of contacts, and more career options than you would otherwise.

Networking can be an effective tool in the job search process for new grads. Not only can alumni be contacted who may be of help to new grads in their job search with leads and other contacts, but professionals in the community where a graduate wishes to work can be approached for assistance in developing a network of local contacts.

Jerry Donahue
Director, Career Center
Canisius College, Buffalo, NY

Understanding the Rules

To effectively network in the college setting, there are several key elements of the equation. They include:

- Proper timing
- The ability to make a personal connection
- The willingness to give before you receive
- Persistence

Proper timing is fundamental to effective networking. The right time to approach someone in a position to help you is not 5 minutes after you meet them or 10 minutes before you need the help. You need to develop enough of a relationship so the person is ready and willing to assist you when you need it most.

The ability to create a personal connection is also important. Someone who is in a position to help you is probably in a position to help many other people as well. You need to separate yourself from the herd to get her attention (and her assistance). If possible, do your homework about an individual before you meet. You may discover a personal connection, a basis for starting a conversation. The connection could be almost anything you have in common—a hobby, an interest, a philosophy, or even a common hometown. These things will help your contact remember you at the next encounter. If research is not possible, be sure to do more than simply say hello to a new possible contact; you do need to make at least a minor impression on them.

You need to be willing to give before you receive. People in positions to help are typically people who are called on quite frequently for assistance. Numerous requests for help with nothing in return can be tiresome, even annoying. If you are able to offer assistance in some way, you will stand out as different from the crowd. It could be anything from offering to work (even unpaid) on a pet project, or something as simple as helping to find a telephone or a cup of coffee. Any way in which you can show your desire to give as well as receive will be appreciated.

Finally, persistence will be the difference between success and failure in your networking efforts. Continuing with the example of the visiting alumnus, very few of your peers will actually follow up after such a meeting. Successful people love to see college students take sincere initiative and will go out of their way to help the ones who do respond and keep in touch. Make it a habit to keep a list of your network contacts and review it monthly to see how you might keep the lines of communication open. If you are working on a difficult class project, you might send an e-mail with a question or two to help get you started. Ask to stop by the office to see things first hand. There are endless possibilities. In most cases, if you've done a good job of establishing a personal connection, your contacts will make an effort to support you in your endeavors.

I also urge students to have a personal rolodex, and (for a while at least) keep everyone's name, address, relationship in it, and KEEP IN TOUCH. As a teacher, I have often heard of jobs that my recent graduates would like to have—but they disappeared after graduation, and I can't contact them.

Phil Hey
Professor, English and Writing
Briar Cliff College, Sioux City, IA

The Professor Angle

Everyone you meet is a candidate for your network. That includes your professors. Many professors have business connections, or even their own businesses. They also encounter thousands of students during their careers, some of whom turn into industry stars. Recent graduates may even call their favorite professors to find out who their top students are. A professor who knows you and recognizes your initiative will not hesitate to suggest your name as a recommendation, even if you do not have the highest GPA in the class. Professors can be a big part of your network-building process, but only if you take the first step—taking the time, effort, and energy to build a relationship with them. A simple visit during office hours (for some purpose other than complaining about your grade on an exam) is an excellent first step.

My advice to students is to take advantage of your environment. Meet all different types of people, get to know your professors and TA's. Visit them at office hours. Set your goals beyond just getting a good grade.

Adelaide T. Auble
Manager, Corporate Capital MA Program
KeyBank

Always keep your eyes and ears open. Potential contacts are everywhere. Parents of friends, friends of parents, fellow church members, people you meet at job fairs, alumni visiting for alumni weekends, alumni you read about in your school magazine, former employers, even recruiters who don't hire you, are all possible candidates for your network.

All the statistics I've seen indicate that up to 70 or 80% of all career positions are found through personal contacts. Typically, career services and the traditional means of campus recruitment account for less than 20% of that number. Therefore, whether you're on campus or ten years off campus, your ability to network is going to be critical to your professional development.

Michael VanGrinsven
Associate Director of Recruitment & Campus Development
Northwestern Mutual Life Insurance

SECTION 6

The Mechanics of the Process

Choosing Your Interview Targets

So what's your dream job?

If you work hard to develop your arsenal of Winning Characteristics, you'll be one of the most desirable students in the recruitment process at your school. Only a small number of graduating students build a truly balanced skill set and a legitimate list of successes. So if you follow the college success model presented in this book, you will have a good shot at the job of your choice.

So you're well prepared, but for what job? What job, in what kind of work, in what company, in what industry, in what part of the world? Interviewing is not much fun for many students and is definitely very time consuming, so targeting your jobs and companies of greatest interest will minimize the pain. And clearly it's a waste of your time and the recruiter's to interview for a job you don't want.

Take Aim

Choosing a profession, such as marketing, programming, or journalism, is an important step in the targeting process, although it's not always necessary to choose just one. If you have background and interest in both physical therapy and dietetics, you may wish to explore jobs in both. Interviewing in more than one area keeps your options open as you learn more about the respective fields. But it will be important to narrow your interests enough so that you can prove your preparation in each field. If your resumé displays a total lack of direction, you may waste precious interview time explaining why.

Defining the direction of your job search is a process, not a single decision made in an hour. Make a project of it for your sophomore and junior years. The more you know, the better your choices can be. Take advantage of all available resources to learn about professions, companies, and geographies. These resources include the placement center, the Internet, and the library. They also include campus clubs and activities, job fairs, and recruiting receptions.

And definitely don't forget everyone in your personal network. If you're exploring veterinary medicine, talk to every vet you can, and people in related fields who chose not to become vets. Personal insights, especially from people you know, can be very valuable.

As you hone in on appealing careers, be sure that your activities reflect these directions. If you're considering a job in public opinion polling, be sure to get involved in related activities such as political organizations or campaigns, and to take relevant classes such as market research.

One of the fundamental concepts students often overlook in the interview process is the value of researching the company. Most people do a good job of researching, but those who don't, really miss the boat. Also, it's very obvious during the interview when someone doesn't know for what kind of position they are interviewing or what kind of company we are. This is unfortunate, because those individuals do not end up interviewing well. They don't shine like they could. Solid preparation can be a great confidence builder.

With the accessibility of the Web, it's much easier to review a company now than it used to be. When I was interviewing, we had to go to the library or the career services office and look at books and annual reports. With these sources, you were mostly looking at numbers, stability, and a little bit about what the company does. But when you see a Web site, you learn a lot about the people and the culture of the company. Then, you can quickly digest that information and use it in the interview to ask them more about some of the things that you learned from the Web site—for example, questions related to the training, the people, or the company culture, etc.

Chuck Davis
Keane, Inc.

Tough Choices

How in the world are you supposed to choose a career when you've spent your whole life as a student? Good question. First off, remember that you are not making a decision for the entire 45 years or so you may be in the work world. Very few people stay in one line of work over their entire career. Job mobility is higher than ever, and talented people prove again and again that one can master many fields over the course of a lifetime. You are picking a starting point, one that feels right and gives you a chance to excel. You'll undoubtedly make some changes down the road.

How Big?

Having said that, what traits should you examine when choosing a future employer? One big question is: small company or large? Large companies with familiar names and big recruiting budgets offer many opportunities, but small companies constitute a huge part of the economy. Each has pros and cons.

Large companies generally provide great training. If you decide on a sales career, for instance, you'll likely receive weeks of sales and account management training early in your big company career. Most smaller firms lack the time and budgets for this kind of training. They will expect you to bring more experience to the job or learn as you go. Larger firms also offer more in-house mobility, meaning you can change jobs after several years without leaving the company. You can also expect better than average benefits with large firms, including retirement plans, tuition reimbursement, and some other goodies many smaller firms do not offer.

Smaller firms vary widely in how they operate and what they offer, and you'll want to get a good grip on the personality of any company before you accept their offer of work. Some are relaxed and have a strong sense of teamwork; others are crazy because they lack enough people to get everything done. In general, you'll enjoy greater responsibility and autonomy in a smaller firm, as well as a greater opportunity for visibility and advancement. Many small firms are extremely specialized, meaning that you have a chance to develop a great deal of expertise in a specific field.

There's no right answer in the question of big versus small—just a right answer for you personally.

Take Control

Every school has its own system for signing up for interviews. Whatever the system is, you cannot interview with every company that comes to campus. You need to learn as much as you can about these companies and the jobs they offer so you can focus your efforts on the most desirable firms. Research really is important, and it's easier than ever, thanks to the Internet.

> *Research, research, research and practice, practice, practice!! Students must always research themselves, the position, AND the company. If they haven't done this and are unable to articulately discuss those three areas then they may as well not interview.*
>
> *Samantha Eckert*
> *Assistant Director, Career Planning Center*
> *Jesse H. Jones Graduate School of Management*
> *Rice University*

In addition, don't limit yourself to firms that come to you. As you conduct research about your desired industry, don't hesitate to contact firms that never visit your school. Just like a persistent salesperson, find the right contact in your target firm and be relentless in advancing your cause. Make sure they understand the level of your desire to work there and the quality of your qualifications. You'll strike out in some cases, but you may hit a giant home run too.

As a closing comment, remember that you and only you are in charge of your career search. Friends, family, and counselors may have excellent ideas about your ideal job, but it will be you showing up for work everyday. Choose your starting point carefully, based on as much information as you can possibly acquire. Changing jobs is not the end of the world, but it's a nuisance you'll be glad to avoid if you can.

In terms of the overall interview process, one of the fundamental things students often overlook is the importance of doing their homework as far as the company is concerned. They come in and ask "well, what do you do?" However, I would hope that they would have done some homework relative to the company and further, that they understand what they are looking for in a position.

Peter Bowen
General Electric Corporation

Effectively Utilizing Your Career Center

Go early and often.

> *A student should visit the career center before enrolling at the university. Why? This should be part of their overall comparison of different universities. The career center can be a key component to future success and securing employment in the end, so it is important to find the university that offers the appropriate services for you.*
>
> *Jim Gourley*
> *Coordinator of Career Services*
> *Washburn University*

Ask any Career Center Director and the answer will be the same. Go to the career center during your freshman year—at the latest. Many will suggest that you go as a part of the selection process of picking a college! And it makes some sense. If one of the reasons you're going to college is to get a better job, it is worth considering the quality of the placement center. How much can it help you get not just a job, but a job that is well suited to your interests, pays well, and will lead you in a positive direction? Career centers tend to collect lots of data about placement results, so you should be able to learn a lot about its ability to help students achieve their employment goals.

As early as possible, make a point of visiting the center and getting the lay of the land. You may not need to use it right away, but the more you know about the place, the more benefit you will derive. A chunk of your tuition check goes to the career center, so you should too.

If nothing else, it's important to learn what resources the career center can offer to you, both at graduation and for summer jobs and internships. Waiting until senior year to visit the center almost ensures that you will miss some possible advantage it could offer.

> *We advise students to start coming to the career center as early as their freshman year, and increasingly many of our services are not offered in the center itself. So what we really emphasize is students' access to career services wherever they might be. It might be in our office, certainly, which is the primary focus on our campus, but also we offer a number of our services on the Web, and we also believe in taking advantage of any learning moment a student has, and most of that occurs in the classroom and with their academic advisors; so our strategy actually is to provide those individuals with information to integrate into their curriculum, in their advising sessions, so that students can have this information on a daily basis.*
>
> *Vernicka Tyson*
> *Michigan State University*

Full Service

Many students are surprised to find the wide range of resources available at their career centers. At almost every campus it goes well beyond arranging interviews with companies that come to recruit. Among the common capabilities are:

Reference library on companies—here you'll find extensive materials on actively recruiting firms and other companies. These materials allow you to understand the business objectives of potential employers, learn about locations of operations, and prepare questions for interviews. Just as employers use resumés to narrow down the field of students they consider for jobs, you'll use these corporate brochures to target firms in your career search.

Internet resources—as an alternative to reading printed materials, you can use the Web. Most career centers can direct you to a wide range of career- and company-oriented materials on the Internet. It's often more up-to-date than brochures, and more convenient to access on your own.

Resumé services—these services help you refine your resumé to best present your skills and qualifications. The level of support may vary widely from school to school, but the more people that critique your resumé, the better. Be sure to develop a resumé before senior year so you're not starting from scratch at the last minute. More and more students are now creating electronic, on-line resumés that allow links to research papers or other examples of relevant accomplishments. Many career centers can direct you to on-line resources for developing this type of resumé.

Mock interviewing—many centers let you practice your interviewing skills. These role plays make you more comfortable with the interview setting and help you prepare coherent responses to the questions you'll hear most often. Every student who has this opportunity should take advantage of it—it will make the first several real interviews much less stressful. Some schools even videotape the interviews so students can see how they present themselves in the interview setting. It can be quite an eye-opener.

General career counseling—the more you know about the career search the better. Career counseling is available at many schools, helping students pick the right profession and improve their chances of landing good jobs. This often includes testing that helps to identify your strengths or areas of greatest interest.

No one can get a job for you, but counselors can help you help yourself to land a great job.

Get Acquainted

Another good reason to visit the career center early and often is to fully learn the logistical elements of using the center—how to sign up for interviews, how to learn who's coming to campus, how to reschedule or swap interviews. Like directions to the nearest hospital, the time to know these things is before you need to use them.

In addition, forming relationships with the center's personnel can only help your cause. You may get first notice of interview cancellations, or other inside tracks to the best employers. If nothing else, knowing the people there will help put you at ease in the often uncomfortable interview setting.

Take Advantage

Career help is provided at no additional charge at most schools. It can be one of the most productive experiences of your time on campus. Regardless of how extensively you actually use it, it's important to know what's available to you.

There isn't a reason why a student could not start to use a Career Center right away upon entering college. Most offer information valuable to the selection of majors, electives, internships, and possible co-op education. There will also likely be a whole catalog of workshops, information sessions sponsored by employers, career fairs, and special presentations on work—world topics that can help any student decide on personal career goals. Probably the number one resource a student should be VERY familiar with is the WWW sites of their Career Center. Most will display a vast array of information on everything they do, when and where, as well as have major critical links to employers and career information sites of every kind.

Dr. Wayne Wallace
Director, Career Resource Center
University of Florida

In the interview process, substance will win over style almost every time. That said, the lack of proper technique can hinder even the most qualified candidate. Below are fifteen techniques that you should build into your interview style to maximize your success.

Develop an on-line resumé. A functional on-line resumé like a Wired Resumé (www.wiredresume.com) can allow an employer to learn more about you than they ever could with one flat sheet of paper. Also check www.monster.com, www.careerpath.com, www.jobs.com, and many others. The best on-line services allow you to link to papers or other academic projects, extracurricular organizations, or letters of recommendation.

Proofread everything. Then proofread it again. Then have a friend who's an English major proofread it. Just one bad typo in your resumé, cover letter, or follow-up letter after an interview will say that you're sloppy and that you lack attention to detail. Take the time. Get it right—completely right.

Look sharp. Appearance does matter. It doesn't matter if your interview suit costs $200.00 or $1200.00. However, looking well-groomed, well-pressed, well "put together" are tremendously important to the process. If your shoes are shined, it doesn't matter if they are Johnston Murphy (or the female equivalent), but if the

shoes aren't shined, the top brand in the world won't help. How you present yourself tells a recruiter a lot about who you are and how serious you are.

Have a firm handshake. It's so obvious. It's so simple, yet some people don't do it. If you have to choose between crushing someone's hand and giving him a limp, dead fish handshake, crush away. A handshake goes unnoticed and has no impact on the interview—unless it's truly awful.

Know the company. With the incredible access to information today, there is literally no excuse for not having some working knowledge of a company you are considering as a legitimate future employer. Visit its home page to gain a general understanding of the company and its products and services. Also visit an on-line news service like PR Newswire the day of the interview to see if there are any breaking stories on the company. If there are, they will be on the mind of your recruiter. As such, they should be on your mind too. If all else fails, read the annual report. It will tell you a whole lot more than a recruiting brochure.

Use the language of the industry. Go beyond knowing the company. Get to know the industry—and its language. It's important to do this for a couple of reasons. First, people within an industry are often so comfortable with the jargon within it that they begin to think everyone recognizes the buzzwords they use. Having to stop them and ask them to restate a question (a better choice than guessing what they mean, by the way), it would be nice to be able to answer it calmly. Second, you might even be able to use the language in a question you ask. It is good to demonstrate some working knowledge of their business, but do this only if you really understand the vocabulary.

When going through the interview process, there are some fundamental concepts students frequently overlook. For example, the importance of quality preparation cannot be overestimated. Take the time to learn a little about who we are and what we do. Don't be afraid to use some of the language common to our industry. Things like that will go a long way toward leaving a favorable impression of yourself following the interview.

Allan Jones
Manager, College Recruiting
American Management Systems, Inc.

Ask intelligent questions. When the recruiter gives you the opportunity to ask questions about the company, make sure you're ready with something more substantial than generic ones. Something along the lines of "So what's it like to work here?" or "What do you like least about it?" just won't get it done. Have two or three intelligent industry-relevant questions ready before you go into the interview. A working knowledge of the company is important to pull this off. You'll also want to know if the person you're talking to is a human relations person or someone who works in the field for which you're interviewing as you develop your questions.

Smile. Be friendly. That's obvious, right? Not really. Students are so nervous and trying so hard to be so professional that they often forget to let their personalities shine through. Companies have corporate cultures—they want to hire people who they believe will have good chemistry with the other staff already in place. If you smile and are friendly, you're more likely to be perceived as a desirable employee—and a good fit.

Show them your "stuff." Bring any quality outputs from your college career or any job to the interview (but only if they're really good). If you have outstanding work, let a recruiter see it. This is more relevant in some fields than others—but remember, a recruiter wants to know what you've already done as much as he wants to know about your future abilities.

Practice talking about your weaknesses. You're not perfect. Nobody is. That's okay, but you need to be ready to talk effectively about your opportunities for improvement. In areas that are not your best selling points, whether it be your grades, your leadership activities, or your related work experience, give some thought as to how you'll talk about them when they come up.

Practice talking about the weaknesses, gaps, etc., they might find.

Phil Hey
Professor, English and Writing
Briar Cliff College, Sioux City, IA

Don't be so rehearsed that you're mechanical. You can actually "overprepare" for an interview. If a recruiter asks you a question and you respond with a memorized answer, you're in trouble. Even if the response is 100% accurate, it will not seem sincere. In a sense, a good interview should be nothing more than an honest, direct conversation between two people to see if there is a fit between them. Completely mechanical answers have no role in that scenario. So practice and prepare—but don't memorize responses to anticipated questions.

Don't be arrogant. You may be tops in your class academically. You may be the president of your student body, sorority, and the student chapter of the American Heart Association. If so, you should be confident—but not obnoxious. Arrogance doesn't sell. It's just not likeable. Just on principle, most recruiters would choose someone a little less qualified if they were a lot more pleasant than you are. Be confident, respectful, and well mannered. Don't be a jerk.

There are definitely some approaches that work better than others during the interview process. At times we run into that student who's a bit arrogant. Once, we were sponsoring an evening function and were getting ready for a seminar information session, and a student bristled up to the desk and said "well what can you do for me tonight?" Obviously, it's kind of hard to make a good impression when you've approached somebody like that.

Howard Roe
Manager, University & Career Center Relations
Lockheed Martin Astronautics

Sell first. Buy later. There are two distinct parts of the interview process—buying and selling. Sell first. Spend your time and energy convincing the recruiter that you are an outstanding candidate. Don't be so busy trying to decide whether or not you'll be willing to give them the honor of your presence that you fall short in selling yourself. You'll have plenty of time to determine which company will be the lucky one to have your daily work efforts after you successfully convince them that you're worth bringing on board.

I think regardless of whether students want this career or not, they've got to present themselves as strong candidates along the way. We definitely don't like to see a lackadaisical attitude where they are just kind of going through the experience, trying to practice before trying for the job they really want. You want to be able to say "no" as opposed to being washed out in the process.

Michael VanGrinsven
Associate Director of Recruitment & Campus Development
Northwestern Mutual Life Insurance

Don't be too informal. "I'm just going to go in and be myself. If they don't like me, I wouldn't want to work there anyway." In theory, that approach makes perfect sense. In reality, it's a recipe for failure. An overly casual attitude can quickly be misunderstood for a slacker's attitude or a lack of respect. An interviewer may translate that into an inability to act appropriately in front of customers. Don't get so formal that you're uncomfortable, but don't put your feet up on the desk either.

Finish strong. End the interview effectively. If you want to take the next step in the process with a recruiter, look them in the eyes and tell her that. Tell her that you're very interested in working for the company and would work hard to contribute if given the opportunity to do so. If you mean it, say it. A surprisingly small number of students do it. Then follow-up with an immediate e-mail to reinforce these points.

Section 7
Putting It All Together

Closing Thoughts

Today there are 13 million students in college—13 million! Yet with that incredible number of people pursuing college degrees, no two people will have an identical college experience. In fact, no two people have ever had identical college experiences.

The reason that no two experiences are the same is that college is not something that's done to you—it's something that you do. It's the sum total of the choices you make in academics, extracurricular activities, and work experiences—nothing more, nothing less.

What you've read so far—in the text and in the perspective from career center directors and recruiters—is real perspective on how to make great choices in all elements of your college career. It really works. If you follow the principles, they can provide a true map to success regardless of who you are, what you're studying, or where you're studying it.

CAREER

COMMUNICATION ORGANIZATION LEADERSHIP LOGIC EFFORT GROUP SKILLS ENTREPRENEUR

ACADEMICS
EXTRACURRICULARS
WORK EXPERIENCE

The question, therefore, comes down to desire—do you truly want to be successful?

Are you willing to muster the discipline to get focused, get organized, and go after it? Are you ready to do the work that isn't always fun—to set the goals, make the plans, and then put in the significant effort to make them a reality?

Most people don't make the commitment, in college or in life. Either they quit before they start or when they hit the first bump in the road. They say that they want to be successful, but their actions speak louder than their words. In the interview process, both the committed and uncommitted stand out to the trained eye. It will be very clear to recruiters which students made the hard choices and took the right steps in preparing for their careers. These will be the students who receive multiple offers and command the best salaries. The others will get what's left over.

So here's the bottom line. If you want success, however you define it, it can be yours—if you choose to go after it.

The difficult choices you make today—to work a little harder, smarter, or longer—will be more than worth the effort in the long term. The difficult choices you don't make will also accompany you for the long term. They'll become your excuses as to why you didn't take a great first step when you graduated from college.

So start immediately. Commit yourself to a great college experience. Make a plan. Make it a reality—and success in and after college will follow.

Appendix
Winning Characteristics Tracker

Keep track of your progress. Use the pages that follow to track your successes along the way. As you start, go back and think about what you've done so far. Even high school counts. You just need to prove you've got the skills recruiters demand.

Communication Skills

_____

_____

_____

_____

_____

_____

Organization Skills

_____

_____

_____

_____

_____

_____

Leadership

_____

_____

_____

_____

_____

_____

Logic

_____

_____

_____

_____

_____

_____

Effort

_____

_____

_____

_____

_____

_____

Group Skills

_____

_____

_____

_____

_____

_____

Entrepreneurship

_____

_____

_____

_____

_____

_____